PUDDINGS WITHOUT

LIFE IN HINTON BLEWETT 1840s - 1940s

Compiled by Rosemary Walker

Illustrations by Brian Walker

FIDUCIA PRESS

2007

PUDDINGS WITHOUT SUET

LIFE IN HINTON BLEWETT
1840s - 1940s

Compiled
by
Rosemary Walker
Illustrations by Brian Walker
Book Design   Roy Gallop and Ken Griffiths

Front cover: A reed pen study of Church Cottage, The 'Ring of Bells' and the tower of Hinton Blewett parish church.

Page 33: A drawing by John Buckler (1834). Reproduced by kind permission of Somerset Archaeological and Natural History Society.

Back cover: A collage of a few of the photographs that are reproduced in this book.

Inside back cover: A Tithe map of the parish.

A small number of photographs reproduced in this book are not of the best quality but have been included for their intrinsic and historical value.

ISBN 978-0-946217-30-4
Printed in Great Britain by Doveton Press Ltd., Bristol

CONTENTS

PREFACE

Hinton Blewett is an ancient village. It may have been based on an Iron Age settlement in the area of the Forbury, including the Church, the Old Rectory and the Manor House. Burledge Common, a short distance to the North, is an Iron Age fort. A local joke says that when the Anglo-Saxons came they could not be bothered to climb up the hill from Bishop Sutton, and that Hinton people are descended from the ancient Britons.

The Walkers have been the core family in the village since the War. Now Rosemary Walker has written an admirable account of the way the village lived in the century from the 1840s to the 1940s, illustrated by Brian Walker. The Walkers' live just in front of the Church, next to the *Ring of Bells*. I have known Hinton Blewett since my childhood in the 1930s, and remember being taken to Prospect Stile, before the Chew Valley lake was created. From Prospect Stile one can now see the Chew Valley lake, Blagdon and across to the distant coast of Wales.

My father was born in the Manor House in November 1889. He was delivered by Dr. Martin, who came up from the Doctor's House in Temple Cloud. He could remember events which Rosemary Walker recounts. Perhaps I can fill out Rosemary Walker's account of the telephone being laid by Bayntun Hippisley from Ston Easton Park to Cameley House, which was then Cameley Rectory. My grandfather, Mr Savory, was the Rector of Cameley in the second half of the nineteenth century. He had been appointed by a Hippisley patron of the living. Bayntun was later a Commander, Royal Navy, and became a patron of the living in his turn. Both men were keen amateur engineers. Bayntun went on to be a significant contributor to the defeat of the U-boats in the First World War. He built the system of radio interception at Goonhelly and other Hippisley huts.

They strung up a telephone line between Ston Easton and Cameley Rectory at an early date, probably around 1880.

When I first knew Cameley House, 'Uncle Charlie' Gay, whom Rosemary Walker refers to, was living there. My sister Anne and I used to walk across from Temple Cloud to play whist during the war. I remember seeing glow worms on the Cameley Road.

Mrs Walker has written an admirable account of a period of which the memories are now disappearing. This is local history with a human face.

William Rees-Mogg.

INTRODUCTION

Between 1840 and 1940, Hinton Blewett was a small, remote and often struggling farming community. The land and the seasons dominated everyone's life as they adjusted to the inevitable march of progress. This book will try to capture, with the help of photographs and the recollections of some past and present villagers, how things were and how over the years they 'improved'.

"Hinton Blewett is a picturesque and healthy parish and scattered village, on an eminence commanding extensive views" - so said a series of Kelly's Directories in the 19th century. It also stated that - *" the soil is chiefly white lias, some of which is very rich grazing land; subsoil, corn-grit. The chief crops are grass, hay and corn. There are fine quarries of building stone and it is generally believed, veins of coal. The area is 1,102 acres"*. The population in 1841 was 336 but it had fallen to 170 by 1901. There was a rise to just over 200 between 1911 and 1921 before it dropped back to 170 by 1931. Until recently, people living in the valley, upon hearing the village mentioned, would say, *"Hinton Blewett, where they make pudding without any suet"*. Whether this was a view arrived at simply to make a rhyme or whether it was an observation based on the poverty of the parish in the past, can only be speculation.

'Tithes' were a tenth of the produce of the land and stock that was traditionally paid annually by the parishioners to the rector. After the 1836 Tithe Commutation Act tithes were commuted to an annual rent charge, based on the prevailing price of corn. For that reason Tithe maps and Awards were drawn up for every parish, detailing the owners, occupiers, state of cultivation, acreage and rent due for each and every plot of land. It is these details that provide the initial information and starting point for this 'look back' at some aspects of life here.

Money amounts quoted are, of course, pre-decimalisation when twelve pence (d) equalled one shilling (s) and twenty shillings equalled one pound (£).

The Good Earth

The 1836 Tithe Award gave the area of the parish as 1,079 acres, approximately 14% of which was arable land, 7% orchard, 3% coppice and woodland and 76% pasture. There were, at that time, twelve tenant farmers and four yeomen who owned and farmed their own small estates. The parson held about one hundred acres of glebe land for his and his church's support; and the owner of the Manor, Mr. Wright, owned just over one hundred acres. The area around South Widcombe was mainly in the hands of the executors of J. Tudor. Three members of the Frappell family owned a large tract of land, mainly on the slope of the parish between Perrymead and Shortwood. The bulk of the rest of the land was in the ownership of people outside the parish, who may have been interested in the suspected presence of coal here. Those owners included R. B. Dowling, a solicitor from Chew Magna, Mr. Broderip, who it is believed was from Clutton, William Coxeter James from Timsbury who owned eighty-three acres, Rev. Williams from Cameley and several people who were descended from former landowning residents. A Clutton charity owned Rachael's Close, the field beside the road on the village side of Sedbrook Farm, and they put the income it generated towards the cost of distributing bread to the widows of Clutton who were not receiving parochial relief.

By the 1870s the pattern of land ownership was changing dramatically. The Rees-Mogg family had become the largest landowners, and their land included most of that formerly held by the Frappell family (who had sold their property before retiring from the parish); the former W. C. James estate that they had acquired by inheritance, and most of the land that had belonged to the Tudor and Williams families. By the 1890s they had also bought the Manor House and its estate from Mr. Wright, and the Manor became their family home until 1902. In total, they owned 48% of the land including most of the larger farmhouses. Then in 1919, ninety-four acres of glebe land and West House Farm were auctioned at the Schoolroom. The occasion proved to be an opportunity for some of the former land tenants to become the owners.

Two of the sixteen farmhouses that existed in 1838 'disappeared' later in the 19th century. One had been in the field behind Perrymead Cottage at South Widcombe, and the other north of the river Chew near the Lower Reservoir dam at Coley. The former was known as Mile's Farm and prior to 1835, in common with Tudor Farm, was 'occupied' by Samuel Jones. It seems likely that the land belonging to the two farmhouses was amalgamated and Mile's farmhouse demolished. The name of the other farmhouse which was at Coley isn't known, but around the 1840s it had associations with a house called Park House that was on the west side of Shortwood Common above Elm Tree Farm. There is a

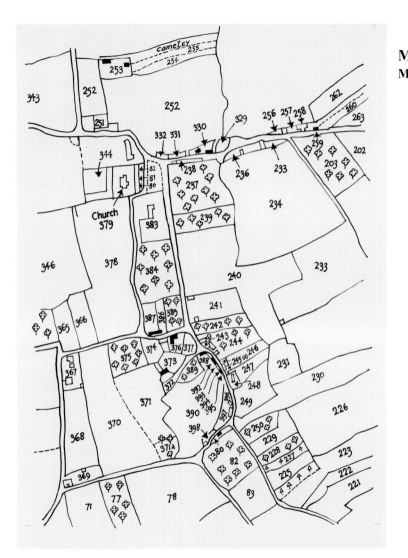

MAPS OF LOST HOUSES
MARKED IN SOLID BLACK

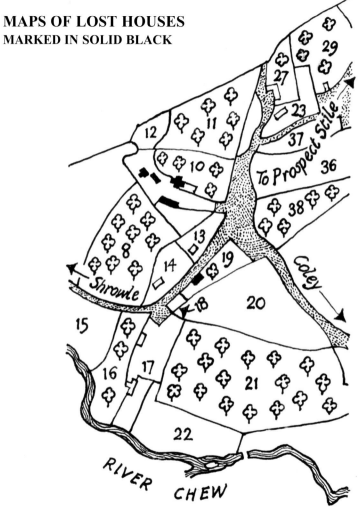

6

suggestion that the farm had been a fine house that had sadly burnt down and Rutter, in 1829, made reference to a 'fine mansion' at Coley. Certainly, as recently as the 1980s there were elderly folk who could remember playing among the ruins when they were youngsters. Others of a similar age could remember their grandparents talking about the days when they were young and would get a penny for opening the gates at Coley and at the top of Coley Hill for the carriages to pass through on their way to 'Coley Manor'. As the site is near Coley Manor Farm and there is a little bridge nearby over the river Chew, as well as signs of a driveway leading down across the steep slope from the north, it does seem possible that it was indeed once Coley Manor. Yet another theory is that the building was not the Manor House but the Manor farm and that the present, listed handsome Coley Manor Farm was in fact 'The Manor' and the classical architectural proportions of the northern façade add a deal of weight to that theory. Perhaps, one day, someone will finally solve the mystery.

Between 1841 and 1891 the number of farm labourers dropped dramatically. Between 1841 and 1871 there were more than 46 farm labourers, well over half of the male workforce. That number fell to 16 by 1881 and by 1891 there were only 8. This decrease in the number of farm labourers coincided with a fall of almost a half in the population of the parish. The introduction of horse drawn farm machinery, among other factors, meant that the farmer no longer required as many men, and with no other employment for them here in the village, they moved away in search of jobs. Some went to the nearby towns, some to work on the construction of railways and some to the local or Welsh coal-fields. Some enterprising young men, like others before them, ventured to Australia. In the parish, by 1935, there were signs of specialisation within the parish farming industry. There was an egg farm at Widcombe Lodge, a poultry farm at Coley House Farm, two cow keepers, one pig breeder and a cattle transport contractor at Shortwood.

The farm worker's 'tied' cottages became redundant too and they either gradually tumbled down or were demolished. The stone was soon used elsewhere - leaving just a humpy piece of ground and a covered well visible. The map shows the sites of these 'lost' cottages.

Almost everyone during the latter part of the nineteenth century knew, as the people before them had known, the names of the fields in the parish. Before the advent of Tithe and Ordnance Survey numbers for the fields, it was the field name that made it possible to identify each and every plot of land accurately. Some names have continued unchanged for centuries, but others have varied slightly as circumstances changed. The Tithe Award and the accompanying map are the earliest reference we have combining a number and name reference for all the fields. The names reflect many different aspects of local history and topography and many are still used today. Some names, like Limekiln and Coalpit Ground reveal a former use, while others, such as Haydon's Mead and Stibbins Orchard serve as reminders of previous owners or occupiers. Some field names include a reference to their size or have an 'Old' or 'New' prefix, while a few indicate the quality or otherwise of the underlying soil. Fields in particular areas often have that area as part of their name, such as Hollowmarsh Five

Acres and Coley Ground, while other names indicate their relative position, like Middle Hill, Lowerfield and Hilltops. Field names such as Butty Piece are a reminder of an earlier 'open field' system of farming and tell us that it was an irregularly shaped, end piece of land that had once been part of the common field. Nearby features lend their names to some fields, such as Church Bridge, Long Path, and Well Close, and the shape of the field is echoed in the names of others, like Broad Close and Three Cornered Paddock. Many elements of the names were derived from much earlier Old English words such as Ham (OE hamm) an enclosure or riverside meadow, Dole (OE dal) common land divided into shares, Leaze (OE laes) pasture or meadowland, Garston (OE gaers-tun) grass enclosure for keeping cattle. Humour is evident in some names too - Forty Acres actually being just one rod eleven perches or about a quarter of an acre! As circumstances changed, the field names sometimes changed with them. Peters Paddock had once been called Abbots Barn Paddock or The Strip, and a field at Coley called Tag had been called Bonds Ground. Presumably because of a sign that once warned of the steep hill ahead, the field named Luke, at the top of Coley hill became known as Danger Post.

In 1838 there were 286 fields of more than one acre. The associated hedges totalled almost 60 miles, and they and the ditches that went with them needed constant maintenance. Growing in the hedges, there were many fine trees that provided shade and shelter for the animals and then valuable timber when they were felled. Keeping the hedges stock proof was of paramount importance and involved a craft that was an essential part of land management. The farmer and his labourers spent many daylight hours during the winter months 'laying' their hedges and digging out the ditches. They set out for a distant field, with their meal of bread and cheese, a bottle of something to drink and their tools, on many a cold, windy and wet day. The firewood that they carried home with them helped to dry their clothes ready for the next day when they would venture forth again in weather that was, perhaps, no better than the day before. Gradually, by 1946, about eleven per cent of the hedgerows had been removed.

The woodland too was managed in order to provide timber for a variety of construction uses and fuel. There is still evidence in Long Dole and Priors Grove of hazel coppicing, a practice that ensured a good supply of wood for making thatching pegs and pliable timber for hurdle making. There was a field called Withey Bed at Little West Close in 1838 and willow still grows in Longdole, so perhaps baskets or willow hurdles were made here.

There were 73 acres of orchard in the parish in 1838 and the apples were used for eating, cooking and making cider. It was very 'rough' cider compared with cider bought today or that made by Showerings of Shepton Mallet when they bought the apples from the farmers. Alfred Gay, of Eastwood Manor Farm, remembered his father making cider at Widcombe Farm and the way in which the farm workers often drank more than was good for them! It was only the larger farms that had the proper equipment for making it, but when Eric Gibbons was growing up at Hinton Field Farm his father made cider during the autumn using the presses that were used at other times for making cheese. One of the last remembered cider presses in the village was in an old shed, on the site of former cottages, in what was an orchard opposite The Lodge. Quite a few people used it because as Theodore 'Theo' Maidment said *"People did make cider then, see"*. Geoffrey Uphill remembers helping Lester Weaver, during the War, to make cider at Glanville Farm. He also recalls the effect that too much of the freshly pressed apple juice had on another of the young helpers! The apples, like the fields, all had their different names: Den Pool, in his later years, would delight in remembering the names that he was familiar with as a child when he was living at Shrowle, *"Vallis, Underleaves, Pippins and two sorts of Morgan Sweets"*. Most of the orchards have now disappeared leaving only the occasional neglected old tree as a reminder. The area between South Widcombe and Coley is called Perrymead, suggesting that the orchards there, beside the river, may have been pear orchards, the fruit being used for making perry. On the other hand a person with the surname Perry may have once farmed there.

Cider, being the local cheap drink, was sometimes drunk to excess and could lead to strange and anti-social behaviour. Usually this caused no more than amusement or irritation to other people. There is a story of someone, who while picking primroses in a field beside the road at the top of Coley Hill heard a man coming down the road shouting and cursing at what was assumed to be a very uncooperative bull. Not being happy at the thought of sharing the road with such a troublesome beast, the person remained very quiet and still, peering through the hedge to watch them both go by. Eventually, as the shouting got closer the man could be seen but there was no sign of the bull. With bated breath and mounting alarm at the continuing cursing, the person watched as the man passed, very unsteadily, accompanied by what appeared to be nothing more threatening than an equally inebriated bicycle! An incident involving someone else who consumed too much cider didn't have such a harmless outcome, according to a story told by Austin Wookey about his 'Granfer', who, at the time, lived in Church Row (now Church Cottage). A certain 'Bucky' S., after an evening of overindulgence took great delight in standing below Granfer's bedroom window and shouting abuse, which not only woke Granfer, but annoyed him too. Not being one to take such things 'lying down', he donned his clothes and went out to confront Bucky on the Barbury. With one punch he sent him flying backwards over a pile of sheep hurdles. *"Powerful man was Granfer".* Bucky didn't survive the subsequent broken back and Granfer was taken off to Shepton Gaol. *"But"* as Austin said, *"they could see it had been provocation and they let him go".* So goes the story - trying to verify it might ruin it.

The mug of cider needed a hunk of bread and cheese to compliment it and the latter was also made on the farms. The cheese storeroom was an integral part of the larger farmhouses with some, such as Coley Hill Farm, having two. Eric Gibbons remembers his parents making butter and cheese at Field Farm from about April through to October, each year. They used the milk from their herd of 25 shorthorn cows and fed the leftover whey to their pigs, so that nothing was wasted. Every day the cheese in the storeroom had to be turned and, when it was ready, theirs was taken to Wells for sale at the 'Old Jail'. Eric remembers that someone would come, with a motorcycle and sidecar, to collect any surplus milk - but he doesn't remember where it went. At that time cheese was also being made by Wilkins' at Shortwood and Phillips' at Sedbrook. On some of the larger farms they began to employ trained cheese makers, usually young women and one such woman was Dorothy Board who came to Widcombe as a young cheese maker. She ended up marrying her employer's son, Gordon Gay, and they settled at Tudor Farm where she continued her cheese and butter making. Some of her smaller pieces of equipment, including a carved wooden hand and butter pats are still in the village.

Theo Maidment grew up at Coombe Hill Farm, which his father Albert farmed in conjunction with Middle Hill Farm where the farm workers lived. Farmer Maidment had a herd of around 30 shorthorns, although Theo recalled that by the 1930s, *"Friesians were just coming in. A good cow, at that time, cost £15 and gave about three to five gallons of milk a day, that 'fetched' five or sixpence a gallon".* He said that *" Cows now are forced - in those days you had to grow your own food for them - grass, hay, mangolds and swedes. There were no tractors then, horses were used for doing things. Haymaking didn't go easy; the knives on the horse-drawn mowing machine often broke. At busy times, like haymaking, friends and neighbours would lend a hand. People helped each other in those days - didn't expect anything in return. Once the hay was in, it was made up into a rick, that was then thatched to keep the rain off - and if the rick was out in the field, it had to be fenced in."* His father didn't grow wheat, so he

Wilf Lyons and his horses hard at work haymaking.

bought the straw for thatching and used spars to hold it in place. *"But then he used pegs"*, Theo remembered. The mangolds and swedes were hard work to grow because they required hoeing when they were small. When they were harvested they were stacked in the fields before being hauled back for storage in a barn

Probably 'Ted' Diamond feeding his hens. In the background there is a thatched and fenced haymow.

by most farmers, or, in Mr. Maidments case in the disused chapel next door. The swedes and the mangolds, which were a lighter colour, were crushed using a hand-operated machine before being fed to the cattle. In the winter Mr. Maidment kept his cows under cover, some at Coombe Hill and some at Middle Hill. For winter warmth, Alfie Lyons remembered his father using dry bracken for bedding down his animals. The buildings now known, by some, as 'Tesco's' that belong to Gordon Wookey were formerly stone

buildings belonging to Coombe Hill that housed a few cows, hens and farm implements.

Cecil Leakey moved to the village in 1928 when, at the age of fifteen, he came to 'live in' at Glanville Farm, to work for Lester Weaver. To start with, his wages were 2/6d a week plus his food and keep, but the Agricultural Wages Board later set them at 4/- per week. He was allowed into the farmhouse to sleep, but was otherwise restricted to the 'back house'. His day started at between five and six in the morning when he would have to go via Hook Lane to the field called Parkwall to catch the horses. On the farm there were about eighteen cows, a bull, two sows, hens and the two horses to look after. He only remembered using the wells in their fields to drop dead animals down! To get cows to the local market at Farrington Gurney, Lester Weaver, like the other farmers at the time, would drive them along the lane to Temple Cloud and then along the main road. Without cattle, Lester went to market in his horse and cart down Hollowmarsh Lane and along Pitway Lane. Even in those days, the last sloping section of Hollowmarsh Lane, before Longdole Wood, was overgrown and they would 'take to the fields' for that stretch.

One tenant farmer, Mr. Evans of Abbots Barn Farm, agreed early in 1917 to end his lease on a small field (between half and three-quarters of an acre) to enable the setting up of allotments. The field, at that time, was known as Field Garden, because it had been allotments once before. In 1917 it belonged to Mrs. Rees-Mogg and is now one of Graham Sage's fields, at Greenway. A private lease was drawn up, as opposed to one under the Allotments Act, and the Parish Meeting agreed a list of rules and

The identity of the men is not certain, but the one on the left could be Albert Maidment and the men on the cart could be the Diamond brothers. They are unloading straw from the horse drawn cart, and the building in the background looks like the old Chapel.

conditions to be signed by all allotment holders. They were:

1. The rent to be paid yearly at the Annual Assembly of the Parish Meeting in March.
2. The allotments to be cultivated in a proper manner and kept clean, to the satisfaction of the Chairman and Mr. Gibbons, or whoever takes their place.
3. No crops except vegetables for household use, to be grown.
4. At the March Parish Meeting 1917 each Allotment holder to

pay his share of the compensation of 45 shillings to be paid to the outgoing tenant. (Mr. Evans)

5. In addition to the rent, the holder must pay at the same time, his share of the tenants rates and taxes.
6. The holders are responsible for the keeping of the gate, fences and ditches adjoining his holding.

Regardless of all these rules, there was no shortage of applicants, but, the meeting agreed that Mr. Hoddinott, who had already been cultivating part of the ground at the top of the field should have that area as part of his holding, but, as it was considered to be the poorest part of the field, he should also have the manure which was lying 'unspread' in the field. In 1918, the rent for each hold-

(Left to right), George Chappell, Charlie Gay, Wyndham Andrews and his father Herbert. Probably taken in 1923. The horses are Bob and Captain and the crop is mangolds.

ing was 11s 11 1/2 d, but, in 1932 it was down to 10s 10d, with each persons holding varying from 1/4 to 1 1/2 pieces. The allotments ceased to be used at about the time of the Second World War.

Potatoes were probably the main allotment crop and in 1918 The Board of Agriculture was encouraging all potato growers to have the plants sprayed. Somerset County Council's Instruction Committee had a scheme whereby local bodies could buy machines, costing £3, and the spraying materials. The Parish Meeting joined the scheme and as a result of voluntary subscriptions the money was quickly raised to buy a machine. Mr. Herniman promised a 40-gallon barrel for the spraying mixture and Mr. Redwood was asked to carry out the work, for sixpence an hour - to be paid for by the owners of the potatoes. The owners were also expected to assist him.

Out And About

The road network in the 1940s was the same as in 1838 when M. Yorke, a land surveyor of Compton Martin, drew the tithe map. Although no roads on that map were shown crossing either Shortwood Common or the Barbury, it was probably because their existence was not relevant to the reasons for the map. The road across the Common had certainly been there for some time before 1847 because in that year a proposal to repair it was defeated by one vote at a meeting of the Vestry. More complaints about it followed until eventually it was repaired, thanks to voluntary contributions.

The Vestry, which was an assembly of the parishioners, dealt with local, civil and ecclesiastical matters and one of its duties was to

appoint a way warden or inspector of the highways whose task it was to make sure that the 'ways' were adequately maintained. It seems that until 1860 the Vestry appointed two waywardens for the parish whose powers included the care of the ditches, at the parish's expense, and the authority to order people to 'make' their neglected hedges. Among other individuals, after the 1860s, Thomas Vowles held the post for seven years, Henry Fear for eighteen years and John Hunt for six years until 1893, when the roads ceased to be a Vestry responsibility.

There were constant problems and wrangles over the repairs and maintenance of Hollowmarsh Lane culminating, in 1858, with the Vestry authorizing the surveyors to appear at the Petty Sessions to dispute the parish's liability to repair it. Feelings were obviously still divided when in 1867 the Vestry wanted to apply to the Highways Board in Clutton to repair Hollowmarsh Lane and the motion was defeated by 22 to 10.

Alfie Lyons told Joan Harris, who lived at West House Farm, how he and his father had carted the stone from Knapp Wood quarry down over the fields to Perrymead, with their horse and small cart, for making the road at Shrowle.

The wide verge at the Widcombe end of Perrymead was a favourite place for gypsies to camp until the mid 1950s. Their tethered horses, traditional caravans and the gypsies themselves busy around a blazing fire were a regular sight. They would come to the village selling the clothes pegs and painted twigs that they had made; and if children misbehaved their parents threatened to give them to the gypsies. It succeeded in making children fright-ened of the gypsies if not in behaving any better! May Watts from Edgehill Farm South Widcombe, which wasn't far from where the gypsies camped, always insisted that the gypsies were *"good honest folk"*

The road along Perrymead, between South Widcombe and Coley, was the only part of the turnpike road system in our parish. It was part of the Nine Elms to Coley turnpike and joined the West Harptree to Emborough road at Coley. It was managed by the West Harptree United Turnpike Trust, which had been formed by the amalgamation of the Chew Magna and West Harptree Trusts, which operated from 1793 to 1876. In 1853 the Vestry agreed to give one pound a year to the Trustees of the West Harptree Turnpike towards the cost of repairing the short stretch of their road that was in our parish.

Robin Atthill, in his book entitled 'Old Mendip' expressed puzzlement about the inclusion of the Nine Elms to Coley road in the turnpike network and wondered if a trustee had a personal interest in Coley Mill. Francis Taylor Doolan, a surgeon from Wedmore was a trustee and had married Ann Frappell of Coley House, at Hinton Blewett, in 1794. The Frappell family owned a lot of land in the parish and may have had some interest in the mill. The information concerning Francis Doolan's involvement with the Turnpike Trust came from F.A. Knight's book 'The Heart of Mendip' in which a quote from Francis Doolan's 1842 will states that he left *two hundred and fifty pounds, secured in the West Harptree Turnpike Trust, to the Vicar [of Winscombe], Churchwardens, and Overseers of the time being, in trust for the benefit of the second poor; the interest to be laid out in the purchase of warm clothing, and distributed at the beginning of every winter to the aged and infirm, men and women, taking care that preference shall always be given to those who attend the Protestant Church and no other'.* So, even if the road owed its turnpike status to an element of family interest, he also showed a charitable concern for others less fortunate.

In 1871 the Vestry had decided that 'the ford and bridge was sufficient for the requirements of the existing traffic and that as no complaint had been received, it wasn't thought desirable to make

COLEY COURT.

A drawing done by Mrs. E. Johnson, the rector's wife, around the early 1870s. Coley Court, Coley Mill, the old bridge, the ford and houses that no longer survive are all clearly visible.

any changes'. One assumes that they were referring to the bridge at Coley as seven years later, in 1878, the Vestry voted for a rate, 'not exceeding one penny in the pound, if necessary, to assist in the cost of repairing the old or erecting a new bridge over the river Chew'. The present bridge at Coley is that new bridge.

The last parish road to be surfaced was the hill from Prospect to South Widcombe. In the late 1940s it was no more than a very steep, stony track and Austin Wookey liked to tell the story of his grandfather's funeral procession from South Widcombe to Hinton churchyard. The bearers had to carry the heavy coffin up Widcombe Hill, slipping and sliding on the loose stones, and one of the bearers, as he stood under the yew tree in the churchyard, was heard to remark to one of his fellow bearers, *"Next person that d'die at Widcombe an' wanna be buried at Hinton 'll have to bloody well walk!"* Andrew Lyons, until just before he died at Widcombe, had lived at West House Farm and Cecil Leakey recalled, *"We brought him up Widcombe Hill in a horse and cart to bury him"*. Cecil also said that as late as 1947 the hill to Litton was so stony and rutted, by the horses and carts, that it wasn't possible to ride a bicycle down that one either.

There was often a triangle of grass growing in the centre of some road junctions. At Webb's Stile there was a large area of grass, and at the junction of Lower Road and Middle Road there was a small one that survived into the late 1950s.

During the 20th century one short 'road' in the village fell into disuse. It was referred to by some folk as 'an old drangway' and it went from opposite the entrance to Coombe Hill Farm to a

A view across the Barbury of 'Church Row', the Ring of Bells and part of the Manor, taken sometime in the 1920s. George Russell's steamroller can just be discerned, as can his hens and part of one of his wagons. The old yew tree that was behind the pub is visible too.

cottage near the back of Middle Road Farm. After the cottage was taken down the 'way' became overgrown and the well and the tumbling garden walls were all that was left.

A new road though 'appeared' directly in front of the pub, joining Upper and Lower Road. George Russell, the landlord at the *Ring of Bells* in the 1920s had, as well as horses and timber carriages, a steamroller that he parked on the green, right in front of the pub. It wasn't long before he had rolled himself a convenient new road!

Some of the well-worn network of footpaths fell into disuse and a look at an old map will show just how many paths once criss-crossed the parish. We can be certain that the paths were there because people walked them of necessity. Their reasons we can only guess at.

Modes of transport changed during the years too, and the photographs show some with their proud owners. Harold Payne, who made bicycles, or more accurately recycled old parts into 'new' ones, was still busy in the 1930s at the cottage that stood opposite Glanville Farm. The Litton vicar, Mr. Pavey, who lived at The Cottage, was one of the increasing numbers of people who forsook their bicycle for a motorcycle. One of the teachers at the school, Miss Elworthy, had a motorbike, and Theo Maidment's

George and Nelson Pool, in their horse drawn cart outside Laurel Cottage. 'Wookey's Barn' is in the background.

eyes sparkled as he recalled the day that she couldn't get it to go. He recounted how, *"Arthur Bishop got on it, the rest of us kids pushed him off and he got it started - but then he couldn't stop 'im. He went all the way up to Gibbons' and back"*.

Steam wagons and a little car called the 'Mendip' were once made at Cutlers Green Chewton Mendip, and there is a story of a car being *"put together by a few on 'um in the old chapel"* here. The proud moment came when the body was lowered onto the chassis for its maiden voyage up the road to the pub. All went well until it reached the Barbury, where it apparently 'blew up'. I wonder what names that car was called during its brief existence? Nothing as mundane as 'Mendip', one suspects.

Eventually, the days of being thrilled at the chance of a lift from the school to the Manor in the Rees-Mogg's carriage, as Greta Harris (née Evans) had been, were replaced by the thrill of sharing in charabanc outings to Cheddar and Weston Super Mare. Then in the 1920s there were 'omnibuses' running through Litton and Clutton and in 1947 the first public bus service between the village and Bristol started. The big city was then within easy reach, twice a week, for all who could afford it.

'Grandma' Holloway, outside Elmgrove Farm in the sidecar of a 1921 Sunbeam motorbike. Her son 'Bill' is on the right with his wife Lilian and their daughter Hilda.

Bert' Diamond with his bicycle and bucket near the start of Hook Lane. What was once an orchard, between Hook Lane and Coley Road is on the right.

Demand and Supply

Most houses had a well or easy access to one, and although some well water was drunk, spring water was preferred, and Greenway spring was the popular choice for the village. On the older maps Greenway Spring is marked as Cadbury Spring and the name raises unanswered questions about its more ancient history. As late as the end of the 1930s, the spring was still the main source of drinking water. Some people carried bucketsful home and many folk remembered the sight, in the mornings, of eight or nine horses and carts waiting while their drivers filled churns full of water. The Norris family at Coley Hill Farm used to get their drinking water, even in the 1930s, from the spring above Priors Wood. Long after mains water replaced the spring the remains of the notice in the yew tree, reminding everyone to keep it clean, was still visible. Water also issued, as it still does, through the wall from the field opposite the spring. There was a time when that ran uncovered down the side of the road, just as the spring water did

on the opposite side. Margery Leakey (née Summers) remembers going across the road from Greenway Farm, to wash in the clear flowing water. When the animals were 'in' they were usually given water from the spring too. While they were 'out to grass' they had water from the streams, ponds and the many wells that were in the fields. The large, heavy stone covers of some wells are still intact but the rusting remains of the winding mechanisms have almost disappeared.

The Cam brook passes under the bridge by the old school, where it is joined, at Greenway Pool, by the

Priscilla Holloway and Arthur Bishop sharing a bag of sweets beside the spring at Greenway in 1933. The notice, requesting people to keep the spring clean, can be seen in the background nailed to the yew tree that still survives in Greenway Farm garden.

water from the springs. According to old maps, the pool was once quite large, so it must have had some sort of small dam across the stream holding back the water. There are tales of it being full of watercress that was gathered by women with their skirts tucked up into their 'bloomers'. When and why the pool was formed isn't known, but it seems doubtful that watercress production was its primary role. Maybe it was for the farm wagons to be driven into during dry weather, to prevent the wooden cartwheels drying out so much that the bands loosened and fell off.

In 1934 Clutton Rural District Council was asked by the Parish Meeting, to prepare a report and estimate the cost of providing a water supply for the village either by extending the mains from Downside, or by extracting water from Greenway Spring. By the late 1930s mains water did reach the village, not from Greenway Spring, but from springs at East Harptree. Laying the pipes up Coley Hill proved to be quite a problem because of rock just below the surface. The hill was closed while the rocks were blasted and the pipes then set in a protective concrete casing because they were less deep than planned. A booster pump was installed on the right hand side of the entrance to Coley Manor Farm to pump the water up Coley Hill. It was many years before all the houses had an internal water supply and that was usually just one tap in the kitchen or outside 'wash house'. Life after that must have seemed strangely quiet in the mornings around Greenway Spring.

The advent of running water provided scope for a huge improvement in sanitation. But even by the end of the Second World War very few of the village houses had the luxury of a flush toilet and the outside 'privy' with its bucket persisted in some cases for over 20 more years. There must have been many different ways of disposing of the contents of the filled bucket but 'midnight gardening' was probably the most common. No need for artificial fertilisers in those days!

The river Chew formed part of the southern parish boundary and was the driving force for the mill at Coley. The mill had been operating for centuries as either a fulling mill, or a gristmill where local farmers took their grain to be ground before feeding it to their livestock. No doubt the grain had also provided the flour for many a home-baked loaf. In 1846 Bristol Waterworks Company was searching for a supply of water for the increasing population of Bristol and one of the best sources was the spring at Chewton Mendip, the source of the river Chew. They built a covered aqueduct to carry the water from there to Barrow, where it was purified before being piped to the city. This solved Bristol's thirst for water but would have left the landowners on the line of the river Chew an inadequate supply for the cattle or to drive the remaining mills, if the Company had not constructed two compensation reservoirs at Litton/Coley. Once the 'Lakes' were completed, a drawing of them and an article appeared in *The London Illustrated News.*

Hinton Blewett was too small to have a sizeable shop but there was a shop at Temple Cloud until about the 1870s, the owner of which was variously described as a grocer, draper, 'flour factor', woolstapler and 'cheese factor'. Austin Wookey's father told him that Litton had a very good drapery, hardware and grocery store too in the late 1880s. So it appears that the local shopping centre for Hinton Blewett was never more than a couple of miles away. Village shopkeepers were mentioned in the census returns prior to 1861 and the assumption is that they sold only limited basic supplies from their homes; but in the 1920s there were small shops, at different times, at Hillside Cottage, Middle Hill Farm, Church Row (Church Cottage), the *Ring of Bells* and Greenway House.

They were remembered as being mainly stocked with cigarettes and sweets. Joyce Harris (formerly Hann) who lived in Church Row, remembered that as a child, she and her sister would be given sweets by their neighbour, Mrs. Jones, if, when they took the pram along the Sutton Road to collect sticks, they fetched her some too. She also recollected that the boys next door, 'Sid' and Seward Booy, would give her little sister a sweet if she went into her mother and said 'bugger' - *"which being a small child she did so prettily"*. Then, in the 1930s, Mr. and Mrs. Fred Uphill ran an enterprising shop at Sunnyside. It was a shop that stocked most basic kitchen requirements and even boasted a blue and yellow enamel sign advertising 'Lyons Cakes'. It closed just before the

Sunnyside in 1935 when it was decorated for the Jubilee. The shop window can be seen on the roadside of the house and the shop door on the garden side. The railings, removed during the Second World War, are still intact on the top of the wall.

war but the shape of the shop window can still be discerned on the roadside wall of the house. The stone used to block the window came from one of the outside 'Privies' at Church Cottage. East Harptree Co-op then became the usual source of groceries and Mary Diamond (née Andrews) remembered walking to the Co-op for her mother, after school. Later, the Co-op van delivered goods to the village and Ern' Dando, from Temple Cloud, also delivered goods including hardware and paraffin.

When Hall's of Clutton and Baker Elms of Bishop Sutton began delivering bread to the village the old bread ovens finally became redundant. Dennis Pool remembered that Hall's had the old-fashioned ovens and always used well water, until they were *"made to use the piped stuff"*. He also recollected that, when he delivered bread for Mr. Dando of Clutton, he had problems getting one Hinton Blewett resident to pay her bill. Every time he raised the subject with her, she would taunt him with comments about the smart patent shoes he was wearing and remind him that she could remember the days when he wore nothing better than clogs! This, he explained to us, was because one day, many years before, his father had come home with three pairs of clogs - one pair each for his three young sons. He, Den', being the youngest, *"got to wear all three pairs"*.

In the 1840s the village had two butchers, but by the 1900s meat was delivered by Tuckers of Clutton, Paynes from Chewton Mendip and Chivers of Temple Cloud. In the 1920s, Den' Pools father, Rossiter was an itinerant pig slaughterer and he would travel around to the farms and even cottages whose residents often kept a pig at the bottom of their garden. Theo, (or what sounded like 'Theale', thanks to that Bristol 'L') Maidment, described how Ross' would poleaxe and then scald the pigs in tubs of hot water, and Mr. Withey, from Shortwood would haul them to Bristol. Den' said that the farmers, whose pigs his father had slaughtered, would save themselves expense by paying him 'in cider' rather than cash - hence all the stories of his father's drunkenness. His father had also worked for a butcher in Bristol and he would walk to work and back via Dundry. Occasionally, when he was late he would walk to Clutton instead and catch the train; returning one evening, by train, he fell asleep and woke up at Radstock and had to walk home from there! Ern' Simmons remembered his aunt making chitterling from the intestines of freshly slaughtered pigs in the boiler in the outside 'washhouse' at Greenway Farm, but on a nicer note he also remembered nasturtiums growing all around Granny Jones' doorstep. Rossiter's sons bred pigs at several sites around the village. They had piggeries on both sides of the road at Prospect Stile, at Hook Lane (where John Hasell now lives), and at the 'Piggeries' (where two houses have been built at the junction of Middle Road and Lower Road). Because the local butchers slaughtered animals all the meat, including mutton, was local - and organic! Farmers could shoot or take rabbits from their own land, but other folk had to be more devious. Alfred Lyons recalled poaching rabbits from the fields above Knapp Wood. He didn't tell us how he did it but many country folk kept ferrets for 'rabbiting'. One thing for sure is that 'Alfie' wasn't the only poacher in the parish. Rabbits provided many a tasty meal!

Many families kept a few hens, which not only provided fresh eggs but eventually a tasty meal too. Frances Lyons remembered climbing the ladder to look for hens' nests in the hay in the barn and being terrified when she saw a face, with a long white beard, poking out from the hay. It was the face of Lamrock Spear who was one of the sons of Angel Spear, one of the village blacksmiths. It was claimed that 'Lammy' had been 'sold' when he was twelve years old and escaped by running away and becoming a bit of a 'roamer'. In later years he always arrived in the village to spend the summer doing odd jobs for farmers and 'sleeping rough' in their barns. When the harvest was finished he returned to Clutton Union Workhouse at Temple Cloud until the following spring when he would make his way to the village again. The first thing he did on arrival was to collect his 'best' clothes from whichever farmer's wife had obligingly kept them for him from the previous autumn, change into them and walk to see his sister, "down Weston way". That visit over, he was ready to begin the routine all over again and start his summer's labour.

There was a person, referred to as the 'Egg Man', who used to walk to the village from Clutton carrying two large wicker baskets for collecting eggs from the farms. He sold the eggs in Bristol. Once a year, while he was here, he liked to prune the rose that grew on the pub wall.

With so many farms in the parish, fresh milk was always available. The children were often sent to collect it and the young Bown brothers, who lived in Nanny Hurns' Lane, were sent to Church Farm, Cameley, where Mrs. Hunt would sometimes give them a bacon or cheese sandwich. *"When it were a cheese sandwich we did throw it away - because of the hoppers in it"*, they said. Their father, when he found out what they were doing, was cross and told them that the 'hoppers' showed that it was good cheese. Looking a bit thoughtful, one of the brothers said, " *Gradually, we got to like it*".

Cliff, one of the brothers, went to work for the Andrews brothers when he left school for three shillings a week. They had about ten cows and used to deliver their milk around the village using a horse drawn cart. The older residents recalled the time when many of the villagers had their milk from George Herniman of Greenway. He took his milk around the village in a seventeen-gallon churn on a horse drawn cart and went from house to house dipping out the requested amount into the customer's waiting jug. When he arrived at the pub the horse would automatically stop and then very patiently wait.

During the summer the cows were often milked in the fields but the rest of the year they were driven, sometimes from quite distant fields back to the farm for milking. Fetching the cows was usually a job for the farmers' sons, and Theo Maidment remembered that his older brother would go, straight from the village school, up Hollowmarsh Lane to bring the cows back to Coombe Hill Farm. Because there were several farmers with cows pastured up the lane there needed to be some agreement over the times that they collected their cows otherwise herds could quite easily become muddled. The state of the lane and the village roads in those days can easily be imagined!

Mr. Maidment took his milk along the Stowey road to Clutton Station by horse and four- wheeled wagon. The road consisted of compressed white lias stones and in the dry summer weather

'Flossie' Porch at Blacknest, milking one of Mr. Shepherd's shorthorn cows.

everything beside it, or travelling along it, became coated with a thick layer of white dust. Milk from some other farms was taken to Hodges Dairy at Shrowle. Mr. Bert Norris, who farmed at Coley Hill Farm and kept Guernsey and Jersey cows, was very proud in the 1930s to win a Somerset Clean Milk Award.

It isn't known when fish first started being delivered to Hinton, but in Den' Pool's young days a man with a horse and flat cart used to bring fish around to sell. One day, after finishing his round, the man stopped at the pub at High Littleton, carefully tied his pony to a nearby gate and went in to quench his thirst. The local boys decided to have some fun at his expense, so they untied the pony, removed him from the cart, took him inside the gate, carefully put the shafts between the bars of the gate and harnessed the pony to the cart again. Patiently they waited for the 'fish man' to come out to continue his journey home. Emerging from the pub, he stood staring in disbelief, scratched his head and wondered out loud, *"How on earth did 'thik' pony get 'imself through there?"* It may have been the same man that Mary Diamond remembered as Mr. Brusher. She said, *"while he was in the village selling his fish he used to pick watercress from the Pool to sell, - that was until he suddenly died in the cart house up at the Ring of Bells".*

It is interesting to note the variety of occupations that appear in the Census Returns. There were at various times: a thatcher, solicitor, conveyancer, butter dealer, nurse, quarryman, County Court Clerk, milliner, donkey driver, coachman, wool-comber and worsted stocking knitter. A look at an 1872 Morris' Directory reveals some of the trades and services that were available in the surrounding villages. There was a tea dealer and tallow chandler at Timsbury, a hurdle maker, horse clipper, cooper and colt breaker at Ubley, a brick and tile maker and a straw bonnet maker at Clutton, a yeast dealer at

Chilcompton and an inspector of nuisances at Cameley.

Until 1902, when Henry Speed became a farmer instead of a shoe and boot-maker, the village had always had at least one shoemaker or cordwainer as they were then called. Henry lived and worked at Middle Road Farm from around the 1870s and even

Mr. Masters aboard his steam wagon at Coley Mill. C. Harris of Chewton Mendip made the wagon.

when Mr. and Mrs. Hummell moved to the house in the 1950s it was still obvious which of the windows had been used for displaying his wares and where on the floor he had worked at his shoemakers 'last'. After 1902 the villagers used cobblers in Temple Cloud, Harptree and Paulton. Some folk must have done shoe repairs themselves, as Den' Pool remembered his father doing. Often, at the end of a long day, his father would spend the evening carefully repairing his children's shoes.

Only once in the Returns is a miller mentioned, although until 1937 there was a mill in the parish, at Coley. Usually, like Mr. Masters, the miller lived over the parish boundary in the East Harptree part of Coley. Mr. Masters and his wife lived at Coley Cottage and Joyce Millard (née Stokes), who lived in the house opposite, remembered spending Sunday evenings with them. Joyce described Mr. Masters as having grey hair, grey beard and whiskers and wearing his cap backwards. During the evening visit, at his request, she would obligingly sing " *Jesus wants me for a sunbeam* " accompanied by her mother on the 'tinny' piano. The only light in the room was from the candles on the piano and the fire, beside which the old man sat smoking a long clay pipe.

There were usually two or three stonemasons employed in the parish, and the stone they worked was quarried locally; a practice that contributed to the subtle differences in character between parishes. The quarries here were relatively shallow and many of them have since been filled in. The one near Hinton Field Farm was filled partly with dumped lime and then, later, with soil that had come from the widening of the main road at the bottom of Temple Cloud. Another old quarry, between Hook Lane and the Coley road, becomes a shallow pond in wet weather and occasionally an ice-rink in a cold winter. As buildings and walls fell into disrepair the stone was re-used elsewhere. Cecil Leakey, while he was working for Lester Weaver, had to haul stones from the disused and tumble down cottages that once stood opposite and a bit north of Middle Road Farm to build pigsties at the back of Glanville Farm. A closer look at some humble buildings and walls around the village will reveal surprising additions of superior 'dressed' stone that must have come from finer buildings nearby, about which we know nothing. There are some such stones in the churchyard shed, built in the 1930s that could have come from the east end of the Lady Chapel when that was altered in the 19th century.

In the 1840s Hinton Blewett had four working blacksmiths but by 1881 there were none. At various times there had been smithies where the garage is now at The Lodge, in a building that was south of Middle Road Farm and at the *Ring of Bells*. In 1871, one of the farmers, Charles Sage, was also a farrier. The blacksmiths were kept busy repairing farm machinery, shoeing horses, making and repairing fire-irons, making fastenings for gates and doors, nails, rims for cart wheels and so on. After 1881, the nearest smithies were at Clutton and Bishop Sutton.

Until 1881 there were also two or three carpenters in the village. After then it seems that there was insufficient demand for a full time one, so Thomas Lovell combined farming with carpentry and William Holloway became the landlord as well as a carpenter and wheelwright at the *Ring of Bells*. In addition to these trades he also offered 'stabling and good accommodation to cyclists'.

Eventually, Mr. Holloway took his tools to Elm Grove Farm, stored them in a shed and took up full time farming. In 1841 there were nearly as many female servants as there were male farm labourers. The other services they rendered were as seamstresses, dressmakers, washerwomen and teachers.

Men with their horses and carts delivered coal to the village from Bishop Sutton and Farrington Gurney. One local, however, would travel to Farrington to collect her own coal. She was Austin Wookey's grandmother, and she would go there with her donkey and its panniers via Hollowmarsh and Pitway Lane to avoid paying the toll at Hallatrow on the main road. One day her donkey was found straying and put into the village pound, which Austin believed was down by the school, beside the stream. Being reluctant or unable to pay the fine that was required for the donkey's release she organized a group of fit young lads to secure ropes around the animal and lift it clean over the enclosing high wall. The next morning the parish constable or keeper of the pound couldn't make out 'how on earth' the donkey had been removed. Back in 1849 a Vestry meeting had decided that the pound should be put in proper repair and that the cost should be taken from the highway rate. It seems unlikely this happened, because in 1850 the pound wall was again in need of repair and two years later the last reference to the pound appeared in the minutes when it was noted that a new door or gate was required.

When Cecil Leakey was asked what people did with their rubbish, the answer was *"throw it in the hedge"*. His wife, Margery, went on to explain that most of the rubbish was burnt on the open fire and what wouldn't burn probably ended up being tipped along Hollowmarsh Lane. A look along the wider verges of the lane, in winter, will still reveal the odd rusting remains of discarded household and farming implements. In 1937 the parish requested a 'dumping ground' for rubbish. There is no record or memory of there ever being one but in 1939 Clutton Rural District Council was asked to supply a dustman to collect the rubbish once a month. On April 15th 1941 refuse was collected for the first time and collections followed on every third Tuesday in the month.

In 1861 letters arrived in the village 'by foot post from Temple Cloud'. In 1875, according to Kelly's Directory there were collections from the wall box at 2.45 p.m. on weekdays only, but by 1894 collections were twice a day and once on Sundays. From 1897 until the 1940s there were postal deliveries twice a day and the box was cleared three times a day and once on Sundays.

Many aspects of life in the village must have changed quite rapidly after mains electricity 'arrived' here in 1938.

No one remembered who had the first telephone in the village, but in 1886 there was a certain amount of correspondence from the Post Office Telegraphs regarding the siting of three poles at Hinton Blewett. 'Charlie' Gay, who moved to Cameley House from Blacknest Farm in the early 1900s, was a friend of Mr. Hippisley of Ston Easton Park and they installed their own personal communication system by running a wire, from tree to tree, between their respective houses. From Cameley, it went via Hollowmarsh Wood and Chewton Plain to Ston Easton. Eric Gibbons can remember which trees provided the support, including one which until even recently had the remains of some of the wire still attached to it. The larger houses and farms were among the first to become linked to the national system and it was obviously a facility that everyone was eager to share. In the severe winter of 1947, when there was still snow lying in March, there had been terrible gales that had brought down the telephone and power lines. Bert' Diamond, of Coombe Hill Farm, had recently had his telephone installed and was one of the fortunate ones whose 'phone was still in operation. Subsequently, when Margery Leakey showed signs of going into labour, Cecil, her husband was sent to Bert's house to phone for the district nurse. Perhaps because of the weather, the nurse suggested that Margery should go to bed and try to forget about it! Mrs. Connie Ford, a mother, friend and neighbour went to sit with her, but it wasn't long before Cecil was sent, yet again, to rouse Bert' from his bed so that the nurse could be convinced that her presence was really required. She arrived in time for the candlelight delivery, with an ample supply of hot water on hand from the well-stoked fire downstairs. Janet Miller (neé Leakey) is the proof of the successful outcome. In 1947, after several years of consultations, an agreement was signed between the Parish Meeting and the Post Office, in which the parish agreed to pay £4 per annum for 5 years, to secure the provision of a public telephone kiosk. It was 1948 before it was finally installed on the edge of the Barbury. From then on it became not just a public facility but also a focal point for the village and eventually a Grade II Listed Building.

"The Best Years of Their Life"?

In 1833 the state began to support elementary education by making grants available to bodies such as the National Society of the Church of England, which ran the school in Hinton Blewett. By the mid nineteenth century inspections of the schools were taking place and a start had been made to train teachers.

In 1851 the three teachers in the parish were women. Martha Pople and Keziah Cook were teaching village children and the other was the governess to the Frappell children at Coley. In 1871, at the age of 79 Keziah Cook was still teaching! The 1861 census gives the names of some of the village houses, so we know that Mary Gore, who was one of the teachers, lived at the National School. The school had an endowed freehold cottage, at Greenway, worth £5 a year.

From the few pages of the school accounts held in Somerset Records Office we can learn a little bit about how the school operated around the years 1874 and 1875. Richard Strachey of Stowey owned the school building and 'remitted' the £12 annual rent as well as making a £5 donation. Benefactors, mainly from

Looking across Greenway Pool, one slightly snowy morning, at the cottages that predated the school, which was built in 1876. In the background is Greenway Cottage with a thatched roof. Just beyond the Pool and on the left is a round haymow, also thatched.

outside the parish, contributed a total of about £30 a year. The school had an annual grant of almost £50 from the Committee of the Council on Education and the pupil's annual contributions totalled just over £26. The two teachers at that time, Mr. J. Cox and Mr. Veale, and the assistant teacher Miss Cox received between them a total of just over £83. Mr. Elford supplied the coal and the total charge for fuel and lights was almost £3. Part of the payments for cleaning the school included the 3s 2p spent on soap and soda.

In 1870 an Education Act led to the government promoting education, rather than merely subsidising voluntary effort but what the village really needed was a new purpose built school. The estimates for its construction make intriguing reading; Eli Magg's estimate for 'masonry' was £64 6s 0d and Thomas Lovell's for carpentry and 'other' was £88. The new schoolroom was to be 26 feet by 16 feet and 12 feet high. Privies and a coalhouse and a yard 30 feet wide were included in the estimate, but not the cost of pulling down the previous building and levelling the ground, which was £15, less £3 for the value of the garden earth. It isn't known how long Eli Maggs and Thomas Lovell took to build the new school and whether the children were excused lessons during that time. A Vestry meeting had resolved that the Churchwardens 'be requested to make a voluntary rate of three pence in the pound on all the rateable properties in the parish, the proceeds to be applied in aid of the Fund for rebuilding the schoolroom'. Once finished, T. Lucy Walter opened the new school on the 17th January 1876 and just two weeks later, over the weekend, one of the windows was broken!

In February that year it was decided at a Vestry meeting that 'weekly payment for children at the school would be one penny, irrespective of position in life, and that no credit was to be given for school pence and that children making default in payment should not be received'. The teacher obviously had a problem collecting the payment because just one month after the announcement, her engagement was under threat of termination *'if there wasn't a marked improvement in receipt of the school pence, which had not averaged more than one shilling weekly'*.

Between 1883 and 1901 the average daily attendance rose from 17 to 41, and the school logbook contains some interesting items relating to the day-to-day activities and reports. The reasons for absence were entered in the book and in 1898 the teacher notes

Pupils, including children from the Pool, Small and Wookey families, and teachers, c1900. The teacher seated on the right is Margaret Comeskey. The boy at the front is probably there because he wouldn't behave at the back. A circular haymow is again in the background.

the irregular attendance of several children, one of whom had only attended 14 times out of a possible 39. In July of that year some children were absent because they were helping in the hayfield - a frequent 'excuse' during the summer months every year. On two days in November 1899 attendance was 'poor' because some of the children had gone to Bristol to see the Queen, an engraved portrait of whom had been kindly presented to the school in 1897 by W. Rees-Mogg Esq. of Cholwell. That portrait ended its days in the rafters of the shed now used as a garage at Greenway House where it was prey to the attention of visiting wildlife and Arthur Herniman, who lived at Greenway Farm, always referred to that shed as *'the one where the starlings ate Queen Victoria'*. The Attendance Officer noticed, in 1900, the case of one pupil whose average attendance had been just two days a week. Not surprisingly, in that same year Farrington Show proved more of an attraction to some children than their lessons. The presence of soldiers in the neighbourhood in 1907 was the reason for another day of poor attendance, while a terrific snowstorm in the same year also disrupted lessons for a day. The school actually closed officially for a day in 1917 because of floods, *'the road to the school being impassable to pedestrians'*. Absenteeism was also caused by childhood ailments such as chicken pox, ringworm, or *'owing to having a great number of bad sores about them'*. In 1899 the teacher decided that one girl should be sent home because her brother had measles and a few years later two boys were sent home *'for having running sores on their faces'*.

The teacher dismissed children sometimes for reasons quite unrelated to health - five boys were dismissed for the afternoon in

In 1877 the school acquired a harmonium *'in order that the children could be taught to sing'*. It did good service for nine years before it had to be sent to Jones and Co. of Bristol for repairs that cost £3 3s. In 1906 it was replaced by a piano, and it's hoped that the children's singing still suitably impressed the Inspector, on his regular visit to the school. His comment in 1895 on the children's progress in one subject was that *'Arithmetic seems to puzzle them'*. In 1900 the logbook notes that Kate Lyons, of Standard Five, had left school because she was over 12 years old and had passed in three subjects, but there was no indication what the subjects were.

1916 (Suggested names reading left to right.) First row, sitting; Peggy Palmer, Mary Andrews, Annie Chappell, Cliff or Bert Bown, Percy Bown, Dolly Chappell, Seward Booy, Hilda Holloway, Bill Andrews, Ron Bishop, Arthur Bishop, Nelson Pool. Second row (standing);? Bown, Harry Andrews, and Leonard Palmer.
Pupils in third row; Gertie Pool, Flo or Ann Holloway, Greta Evans, Ivy Bishop, Fred Andrews, Margaret Redwood, Kathy Bessant, Flo or Hilda Holloway, Rene Chappell. The teacher standing to the left of Greta Evans is Mrs. Evans.
Boys in the back row; ? Palmer, Wyn Andrews, Maurice Herniman in his mothers arms, Dennis Gibbons, ? Bown, ? Palmer. Mrs Page is the lady wearing a hat on the right of the back row, Mr. Page is on the right at the back and Dora Harris, one of the teachers, is standing in front of him.

Although few of the ex-pupils we spoke to could remember anything about a school bell, there is a record of one being hung in 1899. Only seven years later, in 1906, a bell with an ebony handle and 26 feet of stout double link chain with a brass hook on one end arrived at the school from Bristol, by way of the train to Clutton.

1907 *'after arriving at 2.15 pm with no excuse whatever and entering school in a very insolent manner'*. Whether the five included the two boys who earlier in the year had been *'punished by a stripe across the back with a stick' for insolence,* we don't know. Then there was the day in 1893 that the children must have relished when the whole school was dismissed because the keys to the desk and cupboard were lost!

Children from as far away as North Widcombe, Shrowle, South Widcombe and Nanny Hurn's Lane in Cameley, walked here to school, and considering the state of the roads in those days and the fact that there were no school dinners, it must have been a long, tiring, and when the weather was bad, uncomfortable day for them.

The children who lived closer went home for their mid-day meal, but there were no school lunches for those from further afield. The daughter of a person who walked to school, with his sister, from Monksilver at North Widcombe, remembered her father telling her that they rarely took any food to school, but that in the autumn he would collect apples from the orchards and hide them along the route, so that they could be retrieved at a later date and used as lunchtime snacks. Cliff Bown, who came to the school from Cameley, told us that if he and his brothers had any food to take to school it was what he called *"up-line cheese"*. This, he informed us with a laugh, was *"bread and bread rubbed together"*. What he did remember with pleasure was the hot cocoa that was prepared for them on the school stove at eleven o'clock. Den Pool who walked to school from Shrowle remembered eating his lunch either in the schoolroom, outside, or when it was cold, in the 'lean-to' around the stove. He also said that the hand-bell was kept in the 'lean-to'. Some pupils, including Austin Wookey who walked to school from Widcombe, seemed to think nothing of taking a walk along the Cameley side-lands during their lunch break to pick bee orchids for the teacher.

As to the actual school routine, everyone agreed that; each school day started with a hymn and a prayer; that there was a curtain dividing the schoolroom into two; that they 'chanted' their 'Tables'; sat two to a desk; and that the fire was used as well as the stove. They had no memory though of the well outside ever being used. The boy's playground was to the south of the school-room, while the girl's was at the front and had a central rockery, as far as Margery Leakey remembers. Everyone did 'drill' together in the larger girl's playground and Den Pool could remember

C 1920. Front row, left to right; Priscilla Holloway, Violet Hann, Phyllis Hann, Leslie Maidment, Joyce Hann, Theodore Maidment, (Ernest Palmer?)
Second row; Amy Chappell, (Bert Bown ?), Stanley Palmer, Maurice Herniman Den Pool, (George Hoddinot?).Third row; Hilda Holloway, Mary Andrews, Peggy Palmer, Edie Hoddinot,Kate Baber, Dolly Chappell, Mrs. Evans.
Fourth row; Miss Elworthy, Nelson Pool, Arthur Bishop, Seward Booy, Edward Edwards, Bill Andrews, (Ken Jones?)

playing a game with stones in the boy's playground that he didn't think they were meant to play. It involved throwing stones at a pile of small stones that were in turn balanced on a larger one. Access to the boy's toilets was from their playground and he said that there was a *"sort of bar"* nearby that they would use to swing over the wall and into the field.

Like all children, they enjoyed a 'bit of mischief'. Once, Theo Maidment recalled, around firework time, a few of them tossed a cracker into the fire and eagerly waited in anticipation - but nothing happened. *"That was until the next morning, when Mrs. Andrews came to light the fire"*! He assured us that things like that were just a bit of harmless fun, the same as when they tipped gates upside down or emptied the churns full of water that people had put ready for Christmas Day. *"Mind you"* he said, *"if we were caught, we got a real good hiding"*. They also blocked the 'gout', where the water from the spring ran into Greenway Pool, with an *'old bag and everything'* so that when the teacher came back from her lunch break the road was deep with water. Charles Bown remembered that they sometimes used to hide the cane up the chimney while the teacher was at lunch, so it seems that lunch times were unsupervised! His brother Cliff told us that if they were naughty at school they were made to stand in the corner and look out of the window so that passers-by could see them. Upon us commenting that it didn't seem a very dreadful punishment he replied that *" T'weren't so bad - but nobody ever went by"*.

Miss Burnett was one of the teachers and she always wore an apron that the children had fun trying to undo without her noticing. She lodged with the Andrews family at Abbots Barn Farm, where Harry remembered her as being a *'bit heavy handed'*, especially when she was helping his mother to dish out the food. Years later, when he was married and his wife Kathleen dropped anything or was a bit clumsy, he would accuse her of 'Doing a Miss Burnett'.

Irene Kirby who taught at the school in the 1920s and stayed at 'The Lodge', was lucky and found romance in the village. She

The last children at the school in 1931/32. Front row, left to right; Jean Harris, Hilda Uphill, George Chivers. Second row; Margaret Dowling, Roy Uphill, Phyllis Dowling. Back row; Arthur Tovey, Muriel Garland, Jack Uphill, Joan Bond, Lewis Norris and Miss Dyte the teacher.

married Wilfred Lyons from West House Farm and they moved to Milton, near Wells, where they farmed for many years.

By 1931 the numbers at the school were so low that after fifty-five years the 'new' school was closed and the children transferred to Temple Cloud. Jack Uphill remembers how he was one of the children who were taken to Temple by Mr. Maidment of Coombe Hill Farm, in his pony and trap before 'Butcher Chivers', from Temple Cloud, provided the school transport. He used his Trojan delivery van, specially fitted out with seats, for the purpose.

Bell, Book and Candle

In the1840s there was a Wesleyan Methodist and a Catholic Chapel as well as the Church. The 1851 Ecclesiastical census tells us that the Methodist chapel was built in 1839 *'not on the site or in lieu of any previous building'*. It was part of the Clutton Union and in the Midsomer Norton circuit and was built on land belonging to James Green whose father had been one of the signatories to the 1805 certificate, granted by the Bishop of Bath and Wells, to register the house of Richard Sage for *'Public worship of God by a congregation of Protestant Dissenters'.* The chapel had free sittings for 70, 20 others and no standing room. According to that 1851 census, attendance at the evening service on March 30th was only 30, whereas during the previous 12 months it was claimed to have averaged 40. Sometime between 1875 and 1883,

the chapel, on Lower Road, became redundant and since then has had a variety of uses and owners. Harry Bishop used it as a cow house. It is now used as a garage and workshop.

St. Michael's Catholic chapel was built at Shortwood on land given by the Reverend John Brookes, Rector of Hinton Blewett, who had married a catholic, Ann James. The chapel formed part of Shortwood House and opened on the 15th May 1806, although the Reverend Joseph Hunt's Shortwood register book began in 1795. There were 31 at the Sunday Mass on the 30th March 1851 compared with an estimated average of 40 during the previous 12 months. In 1883 a new catholic church at East Harptree replaced the chapel, although the priests continued to live at Shortwood House until about 1900. Much more of the fascinating history of the chapel and its priests can be found in Gill Hogarth's book *'The Thread of Faith'.*

The church of St. Margaret's was dedicated to All Saints (All Hallows) until sometime between 1905 and 1910 when its name was changed by the Rev. James Johnson, because, it is thought, of his wife's Scottish connections. According to the 1851 Ecclesiastical census there were 155 free sittings plus 25 others and the estimated number attending Divine service was 100. It gave 50 as the usual average attendance at morning service and 100 at the afternoon service. A remark on the census return states that *'all the inhabitants occasionally attend at the parish church - except the Catholics.'*

The Rector chaired the Vestry meetings, which took place in the church vestry room, which is now the side chapel. It had a door into the churchyard and a window on the east side, to the north of the door. There was a chimney on the northeast corner so presumably it had a fireplace. In 1879 a new oak lintel was fitted above the doorway that was between the vestry room and the chancel. From 1894, civil matters were dealt with at the annual parish

The view of the church drawn from the southeast by John Buckler in 1834. It clearly shows the door, window and chimney of the vestry room.

meeting leaving the Vestry to attend to only ecclesiastical concerns. After 1920 parochial church councils replaced the Vestry. The 1919 Vestry meeting was the last one to be held in the vestry room as the 1920 meeting was minuted as being held in the tower.

The annual Vestry meeting always set the rate required from the

parishioners to keep the church in a reasonable state of repair and, among other things, repairs were constantly needed to the lead roof, the bells and the leaky windows.

Local workmen whitewashed the church interior walls fairly regularly until at least 1903. In 1843 Mr. Dowling had received 2 shillings and 6 pence for 'fetching 2 quarters of lime for whitewashing' and in 1848 Richard Harris was paid £1. 8s. 4d for whitewashing. The lime had cost 3 shillings and the whitewash brush one shilling and sixpence. In 1858 part of one of the walls was set aside for *'printing the Commandments'*. It cost £1.8s.0d to prepare the surface and £4.1s.9d for Mr Weekes to do the skilled lettering. Interestingly, the churchwarden's accounts show how much was paid for beer for the workmen; in 1843 two shillings and three pence was paid for beer when the vane was put on the tower but only one shilling was paid for the removal of stones and lead from the roof. In 1854, men were paid two shillings for cutting down trees and two shillings and sixpence for hauling them away whereas four shillings was spent on their beer.

The church was heated by a series of coal or coke stoves that were kept well polished, judging by the amount of money spent on black lead. Mrs. Rees-Mogg gave the new stove that was installed in 1901. The fuel was stored on the north side of the tower until 1930 when the coal shed, near the west church gate, was built. There was a time in 1895 when it was thought that the clerk and sexton, Mr. C. Lovell, was going to resign. However, when he failed to do so, he needed reminding that *'the warming of the church should be attended to early on a Sunday morning to ensure that it was warm in time for services'*

The church was lit originally by candles and then lamps, which in 1908 needed renewing *'to increase the brightness'*. There was in the belfry, for many years, an inexplicable long length of brass pipe in the shape of a walking stick with the remains of a rubber car horn bulb at the straight end. The mystery about its possible use was solved one day when a short elderly lady visiting the church explained that her boyfriend had made her the *'contraption'* because she had experienced difficulty in extinguishing the very high candles, at the end of services. Armed with her innovative snuffer her short stature was no longer a problem.

Until 1893, there was a gallery for the choir at the west end of the church. The corbels that supported it are still there and a very worn or chamfered edge on the arch nearest the tower (between the main body of the church and the north aisle) seems to indicate that access to the gallery was from some sort of stairs in the north aisle. To save too many headaches, 'rounding off' the freestone arch would have been a relatively simple job. On a photograph taken of men attending a bell ringers meeting in the early 1920s, there is a crudely blocked up small window visible on the outside of the south wall, near the tower that would have provided a little extra daylight to the gallery. In 1907 a meeting was called 'to consider the question of taking steps to improve the music in the Parish Church'. It seems clear where the Vestry thought the problem lay because they gave notice to Mr. R. *'that the present arrangements of the church choir and his services as organist would cease at the end of that month'*. Mr. Watts, his successor, was paid four shillings each Sunday for playing the organ. Young boys could earn a few pence while attending services by 'blowing the organ'. In the early 1900s they were paid approximately

11 shillings every six months. Dora Harris, who lived in the cottage at the top of Sutton Hill, played the organ and then the harmonium for many years in the early part of the twentieth century.

There are frequent references in the churchwarden's accounts to the cost incurred in maintaining the five bells. In both 1844 and 1845, a four-penny rate had to be 'raised' for repairing the framework of the bells *'where absolutely necessary'*. In the 1930s the bell chamber was in such a bad state of repair that the bells weren't safe to ring. Prior to 1840, on the 5th November, the bell

A drawing of the church by S. Loxton done in the early 1900s. It shows how the east aspect of the vestry room had changed and gives us a glimpse of the large yew tree that was at the back of the pub.

ringers had been paid a total of 5 shillings - that was one shilling each, a year, or a penny a month! From then on they weren't paid anything. The ringing chamber was until quite recently at ground level and divided from the church by a heavy curtain. Until not long before his death in 1972, Frederick (Fred) Andrews had been ringing, mainly as captain of the tower, for more than 50 years and had patiently encouraged and taught generations of young villagers to master the technique of bell ringing. When he died, bell ringers from all around came to his funeral and took turns, after the burial, to ring a long and joyous tribute to him. Ringing practice was held one evening a week, which perhaps wasn't always popular with the people living nearby. Mrs. Wall, once the landlady of the *Ring of Bells*, obviously either enjoyed the sound of the bells or accepted it as a reassuring sound of village life because Gordon Gay told of how, even when she was very ill in bed with pneumonia, she insisted that the ringers were not, on her account, to refrain from ringing in the New Year as usual.

Over the years many of the old graves were levelled, many of the dilapidated gravestones removed and the paths remade. In 1862 George Broad was paid four shillings and sixpence for his three days work making a path for which the eleven yards of edging stones had cost three shillings and eight pence. The path itself was made up of broken stones, which, in 1887, had cost 3s. 6p. to break. Weeding the path was another expense, and a laborious job for someone, until in 1906 chemicals arrived on the scene and weed killer was first used on the paths at a cost of two shillings a gallon.

Mr. R.Hart-Davies Esq., a former M.P. of Bristol, presented the

Iron Gate that is at the west entrance to the churchyard. It had once belonged to the old Exchange or Tolzey in Bristol, which was the place where the merchants assembled for business. Frank

The bride (Kate Baber) and groom (Reg' Hunt), at Cameley church, handing over money to local boys in order to get them to untie the church gate. This tradition still continues here but the money is usually thrown over the gate for the children to scramble for.

Lyons hung the gate in 1899 and in total was paid £2.15s.0d *'for repairing the churchyard wall, next to the road, and erecting the two pillars at the gate'*. There is a tradition here of children tying the church gates while a wedding service is in progress and only when the best man throws a handful of loose change over the gate for the children to scramble for, will the gate be untied and the wedding party allowed to leave. In the southeast corner of the churchyard, just behind the pub, there was a very large yew tree that was believed to date from the time of Henry VIII. It was there until sometime after 1932 and the rotting remains of the large trunk were still visible in the 1950s. Until 1937 when Mr. Church of the Manor gave part of his field to the church, the churchyard boundary ran north from near the Iron Gate to the corner of the Manor garden wall.

In general, changes to the church were gradual, but every now and again there was a sudden surge in activity. One such occasion was after the service held on the 17th July 1887, when *' a Terrific Storm passed over the Church, attended with severe Thunder and Lightning striking the Vane and Tower, part of which fell on the Church Roof with a tremendous crash doing considerable Damage to the Church and Tower'*. A special meeting was called to raise funds for the repairs and a 'Voluntary Subscription List opened comprising all Land Owners and Occupiers Resident and non Resident connected with the said Parish'. The resulting contributions, including the collection at Harvest Thanksgiving raised £101 11s 0d, which was £2.16s. 0d. more than was required. It was another twelve years before a lightning conductor was fitted at a cost of 12s. 6d!

The 5th September Vestry minutes of 1893 noted that *'the Restoration of the Chancel, and the alterations and improvements in the Nave were completed. The Chancel flooring has been raised eight inches and encaustic tiles laid down and the space within the Altar Rails also raised eight inches. Steps of blue lias stone have been fixed between the Nave, and the Organ Chamber, and the Chancel. The Choir Stalls, Prayer Desk and lectern are all of unvarnished oak. The Pulpit and upper sittings in the Nave have been restored, and the large beautiful Western Arch brought into view, by the removal of the Gallery. The Font is restored to its original position.'* It appears that all this work had been proposed at a Vestry meeting, by the rector, Rev. A. Reece only a month earlier, and then just a week after the completion of the work the church was full for the re-consecration by Bishop Lord Arthur C. Hervey. Following the service the clergy and most of the congregation went to the Rectory for tea.

The next major alteration to the church was carried out in the 1920s, but prior to that, there were several new acquisitions for the church. Among them were the two mission chairs, which were bought for 5s. 10d. in 1909 and a hymn board and numbers that Mrs. Page supplied in 1913 for 15s..

When Edward Marriott became the incumbent, in 1922, he took on a church that was deemed to be unsafe and dangerous. The 15th century 'wagon' nave roof was badly infected by deathwatch beetle and was spreading and pushing the south wall out at an alarming rate. It was far too badly damaged to repair so a new nave roof had to be built. Fortunately, sufficient fragments of the old roof were in good enough condition to enable the mouldings and carvings of the wall plates and ribs to be copied in the new roof. Charlie Gay and Edward Gibbons gave the eighteen 'home grown' oak trees required for the roof timbers. Commander Hippesley of Ston Easton Park gave the use of his sawmill and the rector 'cured' the timber. The walls, in some places, were taken almost down to the ground and rebuilt. Dressed stones found during the rebuilding indicated the presence of an earlier narrower

Norman chancel arch, and the ancient rood loft stairway was discovered. The stone altar slab that is in the Lady Chapel was found under the floor of the main church, and the Archdeacon, when he saw it in its new position pointed out that a stone altar was quite

This photograph of the church was taken during the restoration work in 1927.

illegal since the reformation, but he thought it was nice to have it. The old lead on the roof was originally from the mines on Mendip and had a small silver content, so for safety's sake it was re-cast in the churchyard. The 15th century pews had layers of paint obscuring the carvings on the front and side panels as well as damage caused by death watch beetle so they were taken to Wells for repair and restoration. Almost all the windows needed new glass and iron stanchions. When the 19th century horsebox pews were being removed the ancient stonewall seat was revealed and, according to a newspaper article, a stag's horn and a 13th century holy oil bottle of iridescent glass were found while the flagstones were being laid.

Throughout the time that the church was undergoing restoration work, services were conducted in the schoolroom. To cover the cost of the work, Mr. Marriott raised about £3,000 and worked energetically as a labourer, mason and builder, often by candle-light late into the night. The churchwardens and many of the parishioners also gave their time as willing volunteer labourers, thus saving expenditure of about £4,000. One man actually employed regularly was a sculptor named Bennett, a condition of whose employment was that he would teach the rector. Jack Dando of Farrington Gurney rendered the walls. The Rev. Marriott seemingly had plans for even more alterations but before he could complete them he was appointed to Blagdon.

In 1932, the Rector, Father Percy, requested that the Vestry minutes list the personal property in the church that was on loan. In particular, he cited ' *the Crucifixion oil painting of great value awaited the restoration of the rood screen and belonged to Mr. Taylor, (solicitor of Bristol). It was loaned for such time as it remained in its present position'.* Father Percy was very 'high church' and one parishioner explained that after the previous vicar (Mr. Marriott), *" it was too great a change and the village didn't take to it - it was like a change of religion".* Father Percy would walk about the Church swinging incense, much to the bemusement of the older members of the congregation and the delight of the younger ones. D. Brooks verified some of the claimed reactions to Father Percy when she visited the church in August 2002. She had worked as a housekeeper for him and confirmed that the locals did not approve of his 'high church' ways, with the result that his congregation had shrunk to about six just before he left, and she was one of the six! That was not the only way that they had shown their disapproval. She remembered how, after a long day away in Bath, she and Rev. Percy returned to find the gates to the Rectory tied and tarred, the front door tarred and horses roaming about on the lawns. On another occasion she said that one of the chimneys had been choked with stones. She generously added *"It made life rather interesting"*. Margery Leakey remembers Father Percy being very good with children and holding lovely fêtes. They were 'theme' fêtes and she particularly remembers a Japanese and a butterfly one, when the Rectory garden was decorated with beautiful butterflies suspended from the trees. He provided some leisure activity for the men, by holding a small club, in the Rectory, with games such as snooker and billiards.

Another rector, Mr. Duggan, ran a club for the village men called the Brotherhood. It was held in the old schoolroom, where they enjoyed playing all the usual games such as darts, table skittles and snooker. All went well until 1936, when it was decided that a charge should be made for the use of the hall. The decision angered many of the men, who argued that the hall was for the free use of the villagers. Feelings ran so high over it that a breakaway club was formed that held its meetings in the 'clubroom' at Sunnyside. Cecil Leakey, who was a member of the Brotherhood referred to the members of the other club as *"General Franco's lot"*, apparently a reference to the nickname of one of their members. Cecil recalled various accusations that were being made at the time and remarked about one member of the 'opposition' that *" He were one on 'em and he were a churchwarden too!"*

As a result of this split in the village there were two separate celebrations for the Coronation of George VI in 1936. How they celebrated at the 'clubroom' isn't known but the Brotherhood had an evening meal at the old schoolroom led by Mr. Church, from the

A full church for the service in 1937 to rededicate the bells and consecrate or bless the acre of land, beside the churchyard, that had been given by Mr. Church of the Manor.

Manor, accompanied by his dog and Margery Summers (later Leakey), who was 'in service' with him. It was Mr. Church's task to carve the joint of meat, which with the rest of the meal had been cooked by a group of wives from the village.

Mary Diamond (née Andrews) remembered how she, in common with other young folk went to church three times every Sunday; services in the morning and evening and Sunday school in the afternoon. The bells used to ring out to summon the faithful and the choir was always, it seemed to her, in fine form. She recalled that the hand bells were rung sometimes too. She particularly remembered the enjoyable choir and Sunday school outings, by charabanc, usually to Weston super Mare.

When an elderly member of the Perry family, originally from Greenway, was visiting the church one day, she talked about the time when, as a small child, she went there with her grandfather when he 'took' Sunday school. To keep her warm when she was sitting on the stone seat he had folded and stitched a carriage blanket, to make her a cushion.

Bearers at funerals included members of the deceased's family, friends and neighbours while the church supplied the bier and coffin webs. In 1899, William Holloway, the village carpenter, was paid 12s.6d.for repairing the bier. Funerals were accompanied by customs that no longer prevail. The bell would toll to inform people that someone in the village had died and, on the day of the funeral, curtains were pulled in the cottages that lined the funeral route from the deceased persons house to the church. Everyone, including children, stood respectfully to attention as the cortège passed and men and boys removed their hats and saluted. Den Pool fondly remembered how a workman in a plough field stopped what he was doing and saluted as they followed along behind his mother's coffin.

Time Off

Life then was much harder for almost everyone and there wasn't much time left for recreation, and it appeared to be the men who had more opportunities to relax. In 1841 there wasn't a school in the village so the mothers must have been particularly stressed, coping with everyone in a small cottage that we would now consider very primitive. 'Gossiping' with their neighbours and going to church must have been their main chances of any social interaction.

For the children there was always 'the big outdoors', giving scope for imaginative play with their friends, but for some of them their childhood was cut short at a very early age. In 1841 eight children, ranging in age from 7 to 13, were employed as servants. The fact that they were living with their employers no doubt improved their living conditions and alleviated the pressure on their families, but they must have really missed their parents and siblings and the opportunity to play with their friends. By 1851 a school had opened in the village, so no young children were then working as servants but there was a twelve-year old masons boy and a fourteen-year-old donkey driver. Children were usually kept fairly busy, and seemingly happy, helping with chores such as gathering sticks for the fire, collecting the milk from the farms, helping with the animals and running errands. Mr. Bown, who lived in Nanny Hurn's Lane, Cameley, used to send his sons to Maggie Thomas at the *Ring of Bells* to buy him a bottle of ale and porter and his week's supply of five 'fags'. She would seal the drink in a flat black bottle and off they would go home, hopeful that their father would give them their occasional treat of half a cigarette!

No time for play for Winnie and Lilian Maidment until the turkey is plucked. Taken at Coombe Hill Farm in the 1920s.

Other than the various clubs described in the previous chapter, the pubs were where some of the men could be found after their day's work was done. Before 1830 there would always have been somewhere in the village where beer was brewed and sold, with gin and spirits often available there too. But from 1830 the Beer House Act made it legal for any householder being assessed for poor rates, on payment of 2 guineas, to sell beer and cider from his own home. It was intended as a way of reducing the amount of spirits being consumed, but probably led to the situation where Hinton Blewett, reputedly, had at least half a dozen houses where a man could quench his thirst. Until 1872, beer could be sold at all hours of the day and night. Richard Frappell brewed beer from about 1840 until the 1850s at Coley Hill Farm, which was described on various documents as consisting of a Farm House, Brew House and Malt House. A business letter that he wrote to Charles Mullins, of Chew Magna, included the information that he was sending him four bushels of malt and three pounds of hops which he hoped he would 'finde good'. Whether he also sold beer locally isn't known. Eventually the number of beer houses dwindled to just two; the Ring of Bells, which is still thriving, and the Seven Stars which closed as a public house somewhere between 1897 and 1902 when it was renamed Sunnyside.

Mrs. Kettlewell, of East Harptree, recounts a story in her book, *'Trinkum Trinkums'*, about a clergyman who, as he was preaching from the pulpit one Sunday afternoon, glanced out of the window towards the village green. *"There he saw a woman going across the "Fosbury" with a wooden bucket of pigwash on her head.*

Suddenly the bottom fell out and the liquid ran all over her. The parson laughed so much that he could not continue his sermon, and the people, who had seen nothing, thought he was 'ranged'. It took some telling to convince them to the contrary". That incident must have happened before the *Ring of Bells* was built, somewhere between 1807 and 1837 on the site of two small enclosures between the existing row of cottages and Manor Cottage.

The pub was owned at various times by the Radstock based Coombs Brewery, Oakhill Brewery and later by Georges of Bristol. Among the succession of landlords, some had an additional occupation, such as James Shearn, who in 1871, was a blacksmith, and William Holloway, who in 1901, was a carpenter. The pub yard must have been a very hectic place during those days. From the 1830s, the Hinton Club, an organization into which men paid a small weekly amount that entitled them to a payment from the funds when they were sick and unable to work, held their meetings there in what became known as 'the Clubroom'. Over the years the Clubroom had many different uses; George Russell, the Innkeeper in the 1920s, used it for cutting chaff for the horses that pulled his timber wagons and at a later date the brother of one of the schoolteachers produced cinema posters there.

Statements from the Quarter Sessions records relating to an incident that occurred at the *Ring of Bells* in 1847 provide an evocative and informative 'glimpse' of life in the village. A man was committed for trial at Wells accused of stealing money from the Hinton Club and the following depositions were all taken and signed before J. Usticke Scobell, of High Littleton;

James Green's deposition reads: *"I am a Beer House Keeper and I live at Hinton Blewett in this County - there is a Benefit Society called 'The Hinton Club' held at my House - I am a Member of such Club. On the seventh of December last I received from the Stewards, Henry Backhouse and the Clerk the Club Box, containing the Money - but I don't know what money it contained- but I saw the Stewards and the Clerk put the money into it. It has three Keys and Locks, one of such keys being kept by the Clerk, and the other two by the two Stewards - I put it into my Bed Room. On the 26th of December instant at about 1/2 past 9 o'clock in the Evening I received Information that the Box was missing, and I then went up stairs and found all the doors open and the Box gone - I immediately made known the loss to the People in the House - and shortly afterwards the Prisoner came in, he appeared to be flurried and from his general manner I suspected him - He said " I hope you don't blame me for it" - I then said "Thou are't the Man" I took hold of him by the collar, and he struggled to get away - I sent for a Constable and had him taken into Custody - The Box now produced by the Constable is the one that was stolen out of my Bed Room - The Prisoner is well acquainted with the ways of my House - he slept for several Weeks in my House last summer - and he passed this my Bed Room, where the Club Box was kept to go to the room where he slept - most of the Money was found next Morning at about 9 o'clock tied up in a Handkerchief under a Wall about if a 100 yards from my House - and the Club Box was found in a Well about 200 yards from my House, all beaten in, as it now appears - there were splinters of the broken Box and a Brick-bat near the Well which showed where the Box was*

A choir and churchwardens outing to Weymouth. Left to right; Mr. E Gibbons, Charlie Gay, the driver, Mr. Marriot (Rector), Mrs. C Gay, either Millie Board or Mrs. Shepherd, Rene Board, Stanley Harris, Fred Andrews, Sidney Booy, George Hoddinot, Elsie Male, Monica Small The six people higher up at the back; one of the Boards?, Mary Andrews, Wyndham Andrews, Ern' Swimmer, Graham Perry and Arthur Spear, the postman who lodged with the Andrews family.

broken open - and a little of the Money was found there - and under the Wall of the Garden in which the Box was broken open, there were foot marks showing where a Person had got over the Wall - there was a little snow there which had impressions of two feet - We found these footmarks at about 11 o'clock - I accompanied Richard Backhouse the Constable and several others and compared the Prisoner's quarter boots with the footmarks and

they corresponded - the Boot of the right foot has it's tip on, but the tip is gone from the left boot - the impression in the snow corresponded in that particular - the Boots also corresponded in length and breadth with the footmarks - I have no doubt but that the Prisoner's boots left the footmarks - I produce the Handkerchief in which the Money was found, I took it to the Prisoners House and showed it to his sister and asked her if she knew whose it was, and she said it was her Brother the Prisoner's - she has since denied it, after knowing the object of my enquiry.

James' wife, Elizabeth's report reads: *I went upstairs to my Bed Room on Saturday Afternoon the 26th of December instant at about 5 o'clock, and I then saw the Club Box (now produced by the Constable) safe in my Bed Room - I came out of the Room and fastened the Doors - about 1/2 past 9 o'clock the same Evening I had occasion to go upstairs - then I found the Room Doors open, and the Club Box gone - I informed my Husband of it. Shortly afterwards I took the Prisoner upstairs into the Room from whence the Box was stolen, and he trembled and appeared much frightened - His hands shook and he said to me "See I do shake and am frightened as much as you, I hope you don't blame me for it" - On coming down stairs my Husband accused him with it - he told him that he knew the ways of the house and no one else could have done it - my Husband then took* him into Custody - he made great resistance - He came to our House between 5 & 6 o'clock and was drinking with the People - it was possible for the Prisoner to have taken advantage of our being engaged, and to have gone up stairs and have taken the Club Box without my observing it as our House was full of Company - the Club Box I believe was taken thro' another outer door which opened to the Club Room steps, and not brought down thro' the House.

Richard Backhouse, one of the Constables, stated: *I assisted in taking charge of the Prisoner the same Evening as the Club Box was stolen - the next morning I took the Prisoner's 1/4 Boots off and went with James Green, Elishe Horler and several others to some foot marks that were in some snow under the wall of the Garden in which the Well is where the Box was found - I delivered the Boots to the other Constable Thomas Lovell and I remained the other side of the Wall, whilst he and the rest that were there compared them with the foot marks - on their pronouncing them as fitting I got over the Wall, the Boots were in the tracks. I produce the Prisoners Boots.*

His fellow Constable, Thomas Lovell, described how he compared the boots with the footmarks and discovered that they corresponded in all respects. Henry Backhouse's account of his part in the proceedings states: *I am a Farmer and I live at Hinton Blewett - I keep the accounts of the Club - the last Club night was on the 7th of this December - I and the Stewards then left in the Box £5 18s 10p - there were two Sovereigns amongst it - the rest was in Silver, with the exception of about 2 shillings worth of halfpence - the Box was locked as usual, and we left it in the care of the Witness James Green, the Landlord of the Beer House - I retained one of the Keys. The Club has been formed about 8 years. It has no regular Articles but is governed by the Articles of a neighbouring Society. The Prisoner was a Member of the Club sometime ago - he has allowed 7 Club nights to pass without paying his Money - I consider him now to be consequently no longer a Member. William Hand and Henry Dowling are the Stewards of the Club.*

Elisha Horler said: *I am the Parish Clerk and I live in Hinton Blewett - I am also a Member of the Club - The next morning after the Club Box was stolen, I found the Handkerchief produced by the Witness James Green, under a Wall about 100 yards from James Green's Beer House. I called to several others that were searching for the Money and went with them to James Green's and there told it - there was in the Handkerchief £5 6s 10d - there was picked up where the Box was broken 101/2 d and I have heard there was 1s 111/2 d found in James Green's garden - and I have no doubt of such Money being what was stolen with the Box - I delivered the Money over to James Green - I also compared the Boots with the foot marks in the snow, I observed the Marks before the Boots were put into them. There was the Tip missing in the track of the left foot and there was no Tip on the Boot of the left foot".*

The accused was asked what he had to say for himself and he replied, " *I know nothing about it*". After serving his six-month sentence, he settled back in the parish, resumed working as a sawyer, probably at the public saw pit on Widcombe Common, and raised a family.

In the account above, mention was made of two parish constables. These men were chosen from a list of possibly eight to ten parishioners who were recommended at the annual Vestry meeting 'as fit and proper persons to serve the Office of Parish Constables' and their duties would have included dealing with matters of law and order and collecting taxes. A village family still has the wooden and brass tipstaff, engraved with the initials H B, that was a sign of the constable's authority as well as being useful for self-defence.

When local policemen replaced the village constables, they cycled here from Temple Cloud where they were based. It was obviously thirsty work and required an occasional quick visit to the pub. One day while one of them was quenching his thirst, his sergeant was spotted waiting for him out on the Barbury. Leaving by the door would have risked him being seen by his 'boss' so he settled for being pushed unceremoniously out through the back, very small window into the churchyard. It may have been the same policeman who suggested to a group of young village lads that he saw playing cards on the tank of Bill Andrews' motorbike that playing somewhere less conspicuous than the Barbury, on a Sunday morning, might be appropriate. The suggestion obviously 'fell on deaf ears' or was deliberately ignored because the lads continued the practice, regardless of any signs of disapproval by the churchgoers leaving morning service. There seems to have been good relations between the police and the locals, whose general opinion was that *"They used to come up, but they never really interfered with anyone"*.

The Seven Stars was built at about the same time as the *Ring of Bells*, but the first time that the name was mentioned in the census was in 1861, when James Green, formerly of the *Ring of Bells*, was the landlord. James died not long after that and his son George took over for about seventeen years, followed by Eli Burr and then Andrew Lyons, who had once been a Mendip lead miner. He was the last landlord there and after he moved to West House Farm in 1901, *The Seven Stars* was renamed *Sunnyside*. Judging from the shapes and amount of broken pieces of china found during the building of Ozenhay, the pub used the traditional

What may have been a Sunday school outing to Cheddar in the late 1920s. Among the passengers are Betty Shepherd and her mother, Mr. Garland, and members of the Andrews, Booy, Redwood and Pool families.

'mocha ware' that was so popular at the time. It isn't known if the Hinton Club transferred its meeting place to *The Seven Stars* when James Green moved there, but it is recorded that the Sequestrator for the Bishop of Bath and Wells came there, to collect the tithe rent charges.

The large ' clubroom' at *The Seven Stars* continued to be used for social events long after the pub closed. Memories survived of the time that Ron Bishop poured water down the chimney when a meeting was being held there and the ashes went all over Mr. Shepherd. Harry Bishop after enjoying an evening in the clubroom, reputedly, rarely managed to complete his journey home to Middle Road Farm before the next morning. The Women's Institute held their meetings there too, probably unaware that the lads of the village referred to it as the 'Destitute'. Dances were another popular event at the clubroom. Before the war admission cost one shilling and Mr Parker, the blind pianist, provided the music. He walked to the village from Midsomer Norton, by way of Pitway and Hollowmarsh Lane, and it is said that he only ever lost his way once. That happened when he stumbled into a cow that was lying across his path and the resulting confusion caused him to lose his bearings. 'Ernie' Phillips who was an evacuee at Glanville Farm with Lester Weaver, 'ran' a cinema once a week at the clubroom. Den Pool remembered it as being on a Wednesday evening and costing sixpence for adults and three pence for children. *'Lorna Doone'* was regularly on the bill and the evening always ended with Vera Lynn's recording of *'We'll Meet Again'*. When he could afford three pence, Den liked to go to East Harptree Theatre to see a Charlie Chaplin film.

Outings aboard Mendip Queen coaches were a summer treat, with Weston, Cheddar and Burnham being popular destinations. Cycling to Weston was another activity on a Sunday afternoon. Occasionally people cycled to Bristol but as Cecil Leakey commented, *" You had to watch out for them tram lines"*.

A village cricket team used to play at Blacknest, when Mr. Shepherd lived there, and they travelled to away matches, at far away as Queen Charlton, by bicycle and horse and cart. The players included Fred Andrews (a demon bowler), Graham Perry, Ron

Two members of the village cricket team; Graham Perry (left) and Fred Andrews, at Blacknest Farm. Betty Shepherd is sitting on the roller and her mother, Florence, is behind her.

Bishop, Cecil Leakey, Seward Booy, Harry and Wyn' Andrews, and Charlie Wilkins from Shortwood, who was the captain. Some of the ladies of the village played tennis on the court that was north of the Manor garden. They included Mary Andrews, Dora and Greta Harris and Betty Shepherd. Memories of the gnats that were such a nuisance under the trees remained with them long after their tennis days were over.

The Church fête was one of the highlights of the year. *"Fêtes were real fêtes in those days"* was a comment often made to us. People talked of how there were lots of things going on there and how the skittles prize was a live pig, often given by Johnny Pool. Wilfred Beer, from Coley, remembers coming with lots of other people from the surrounding villages to enjoy the excitement of the afternoon and he still treasures the Victorian figurines that he won on the spinning jenny, despite his mother accusing him of bringing home more rubbish! Harvest Home celebrations were another feature of the year. According to the minutes of the Parish Meeting in 1920, a free tea was planned for all the children in a tent measuring 70 by 25 feet that had cost £6 to hire, and a band was to be hired too. Adults were to be charged 1s. 9d if they went to the tea and the dance, or 1s. if they only went to the dance.

A diary written by Lord Rees- Mogg's father, when he was living with his parents at the Manor in the early 1900s, reveals a few more of the pastimes enjoyed by some of the locals. In August 1900, for instance, Clutton held its Annual Show with cycle racing as one of the events and W. Edmonds, who was the amateur champion of England over one mile, was one of the competitors. There was no mention in the diary of a Hinton Blewett rival.

William, the writer of the diary, shared his hobby of catching and collecting butterflies with Arthur Johnson from the Rectory and he listed some of the species that he caught while on picnics at Widcombe and 'Burleigh' Common There were Pale Brimstones, Peacocks and Painted Ladies as well as others that he didn't specify. He also wrote about the time that Bessie Flower, who was their gardener's wife, held a tea party on the Manor lawn for 50 parish workers from Bristol. After the tea the festivities continued at Prospect Stile where they all joined in singing seven hymns.

Anna Johnson, the Rector's daughter, spent much of her time researching and writing two books based on local folk tales and historical events. The first was *'Haydon's Gully'*, a tale about Major Haydon, a Cavalier Officer and son of a Widcombe farmer, who evaded his pursuers during the Civil War by hiding in a cavern in the side of a deep gully formed by the stream that runs down from Spring Lane, near Prospect Stile. The second tale, *'Harptree Coombe'*, was written soon afterwards and was based on the story of Richmond Castle in East Harptree. It was set in the 12th century, when King Stephen's army besieged the castle belonging to William the 'Baron de Harptrew' who was loyal to Queen Maud.

Seward Booy had a pair of village quoits that each weighed two pounds. He couldn't remember quoits being played in his time, but said that he had been told that it used to be played on the Barbury. To play the game a bed of clay was laid down and a four feet square marked out on it using oak headstocks. An iron pin, about an inch across, was driven into the clay until it was flush with the surface and each player had a pair of iron quoits that could each weigh anything up to 12 pounds. The aim was to throw the quoits from a distance of 18 feet and try to get them as near the pin as possible with the help of a partner who indicated the exact position of the pin by inserting small pieces of paper into the clay. It was a very popular competitive game but there is no record of the village ever having had a team in the local leagues. Quoits had a reputation for being associated with a large intake of beer, which a photograph of the East Harptree team and Austin Wookey's memories do nothing to dispel.

Alice Rawlings of Abbots Barn Farm in fancy dress with her bicycle, probably off to the church fête. The photograph was taken about 1900.

Care in the Community

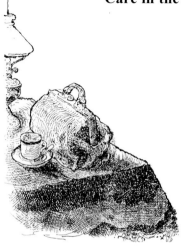

It may be tempting to yearn for some of the aspects of life in those far off years, between 1840 and the 1940s, but one aspect that is not to be envied is the standard of health care.

In July 1849 a Vestry meeting was called because of the 'near approach of the Cholera'. The knowledge of an earlier epidemic of Asian cholera that had left 72 people dead in Paulton in 1832 must have reminded everyone of the serious consequences if another epidemic broke out, so a prompt response was initiated. A seven-man committee was appointed to *'inspect the parish for the purpose of causing Nuisances to be abated, the Houses whitewashed and anything else deemed requisite'*. The same routine was followed again in 1853 when another outbreak occurred locally, but fortunately the whitewash here wasn't put to the test on either occasion.

Mention has already been made of the infectious diseases and ailments from which children in particular suffered. The 'treatments' used for many ailments were mainly ones that had been used for generations and included the use of particular plants and even animal parts. In her book *'Trinkums Trinkums'* Mrs. Kettlewell wrote about an amusing cure that was described to her by the granddaughter of a Hinton Blewett Rector. It concerned a woman whose cow was very ill and who begged a neighbouring vicar, who was visiting the parish, to cure it for her. She was so insistent that, at last, he consented to do his best. He took his stick and solemnly made a circle around the cow saying, *"If she lives, she lives. If she dies, she dies"*. Fortunately the cow recovered, but sometime later the vicar himself fell ill with quinsy and it was feared that he might choke. When the woman whose cow had been cured heard this, she insisted on visiting his room because of a cure that she knew. She pulled out his bed and proceeded to walk solemnly round it saying, *"If he lives, he lives. If he dies, he dies"*. The vicar suddenly recalled the time that he had said the very same thing and the combination of that memory and the woman's actions amused him so much that he burst out laughing. The movement broke the quinsy and he recovered!

The parish burial registers reveal that infant mortality was disturbingly high, with many of the entries being for babies who had only managed to cling on to life for a few days. The names of young children and children in their 'teenage' years also frequently appear in the registers and it is probably fair to assume that if they had enjoyed the same housing conditions, free access to a doctor and the subsequent healthcare that is available to us today, most of their young lives would have been spared. Three of Andrew and Alice Lyons' children died of diphtheria in 1903 within the space of five days. Edith died on 5th July aged seven, and five-year-old Edgar and eleven-year-old Amy died on 10th July. They were all buried in the churchyard, near the belfry door, on the day following their deaths.

William W. Rees-Mogg became very active on behalf of the village, in 1902, when Clutton Rural District Council announced plans to open an 'infectious hospital' here. The house that they proposed using was The Lodge, which had been offered by Mr. Pollett of Temple Bridge at a yearly rent of nine pounds for a period of 7, 14, or 21 years. The lease was drawn up and efforts made

The Lodge in the late 1930s.

to find someone to take charge of the premises. There was a slight delay when a suitable pauper couldn't be found for the job and someone else had to be sought. After receiving a letter of objection from Mr. Rees-Mogg they notified him that the lease had already been drawn up and that the letter had arrived too late to affect the matter. In response to this, Mr. Rees-Mogg threatened them with an injunction unless they abandoned the idea of using that house. On that same day, the Clerk to the District Council pointed out that cases of smallpox and other infectious diseases had been successfully isolated in the cottages in the Workhouse grounds, *'which were much nearer to an inhabited house than the Hinton Blewett house and about the same distance from the road'*. The Council next decided to seek the opinion of the Medical Officer of Health, but noted that Henry Payne lately of the Fir Tree Inn, Midsomer Norton was willing to take charge of the house for a small weekly payment. After the Council received the letter from the Medical Officer stating that in the case of smallpox being retained in the house in question there would be a very great danger of the disease being communicated to the inhabitants of the nearest house, they informed Mr. Rees-Mogg that the house here in the village would, after all, not be used. A great sigh of relief must have swept around the village.

There have always been tragic accidents and a poignant entry in the Burial Register for February 14th 1870 tells us of the consequences of one. On that day, 75-year-old George Barwell was buried and the rector noted that he had died suddenly. But, also on that day James Jones who was George's four-year-old grandson was buried. The entry beside his name in the register was 'burnt to death in a fire'.

A Chewton Mendip Doctor's books, covering the beginning of the 20th century reveal some of the ailments suffered by the local population and the cost of the medical attention 'given'. One unfortunate man who had been kicked in the face by a horse was charged five shillings for the assistance of the doctor, and the parents of a child who needed his thumb splint re-applied were charged one shilling and sixpence. Another fellow had to suffer the indignity of having his buttock sutured and then 'put his hands in his pocket' for the three shillings and sixpence fee. If toothache

happened to be the problem the doctor would, for two shillings and six pence, come and extract it, although 'Payne's child' had a tooth removed for only one shilling. Three shillings and sixpence seemed to cover the cost of quite a variety of treatments including having an enema at home, an ear syringed or a leg wound dressed. On the maternity scene, the heartbreak of a miscarriage resulted in a bill for one guinea and the expert attention required for a forceps delivery, two guineas. Not all patients were able or prepared to settle their accounts and comments like' bad lot gone away' appeared beside some names. A man from Widcombe obviously came to a mutually beneficial way of settling his account because against his name the amount was ticked off and 'by butter' written beside it. Between 1899 and 1921, a total of 43 families from the parish had benefited from the attentions of the Chewton Mendip doctor at one time or another. The daily details of his practice showed the diversity of the problems he dealt with and the distances he travelled. That, combined with his meticulous bookkeeping, leaves one with a great deal of admiration for his energy, and respect for his expertise. One person was pleasantly and unexpectedly surprised, while reading through the Doctor's accounts book, to stumble across entries for her grandparents. One entry showed that the cost of a confinement had been one guinea, attention for the mother had been ten shillings and sixpence and for the baby two shillings, a total of £1 13s 6d. A closer look at the date beside it revealed that it was the cost for the safe delivery of her father.

Before the Poor Law Amendment Act of 1834 the Vestry of each parish had been responsible for making arrangements to aid its poor and needy. The Act aimed to standardise the support given

Cambrook House, known earlier as Clutton Union Workhouse, which opened in 1838.

to paupers by grouping parishes together into Unions that would have an appropriately staffed Workhouse and set the poor rate for the whole area. The Clutton Union covered twenty-nine parishes, including Hinton Blewett and parishes as far apart as Radstock and Nempnett Thrubwell. Their Workhouse was built in Eastcourt Road, Temple Cloud and in 1836 the contract to build it was given to James Parfitt of Clutton and Richard Kennard of East Harptree. They were given twelve months to complete the task at a cost of £4,950. Each parish had to contribute to the cost of the building but continue to collect its poor rate. In return, the parishioners were eligible for assistance from the Union either in the form of out-relief payments, donations of clothes and food, or as residents in the workhouse. One, seemingly very harsh reality for the families that went to the workhouse was that they were split up because men, women and children were housed separately. To make sure that the spiritual and educational needs of the inmates were taken care of, the workhouse had a chapel and a room for the children's schooling. Inmates had to do a variety of tasks, including gardening, cleaning and sewing. As each workhouse was expected to be partially self-supporting there was also work to be done in their bakery, laundry and on the small farm.

Apart from the individuals and families for whom life was proving financially difficult, quite a few of our elderly, widowed, or unmarried men ended their lives in the workhouse. 'Lammy' Spear was one such person and despite his seemingly hard life he lived until he was in his eighties.

Tramps were kept apart from the other inmates in 'Casual Wards', where they were only accepted if they had obtained a form of authority from the local police station. On arrival in the workhouse they had to bath before they were given an evening meal, bed and breakfast and a meal voucher that could be

A photo of 'Lammy' Spear, probably at The Seven Stars in the 1890s, when he was Andrew Lyons' servant. He died in the workhouse in 1925 but was buried here in the churchyard.

exchanged for a small amount of bread and cheese from a local shop. But, before leaving the next morning they had to perform a task such as chopping firewood or breaking stones that had been fetched from a local quarry.For many years the workhouse operated with fewer than 10 paid staff caring for anything up to 150 inmates.

Inevitably there were sometimes rumblings of discontent from the various parishes. In 1843, our Vestry met to *'consider the necessity of reducing the salaries of all the officers of the Clutton Union in consequence of the lessened price of provisions and consequent reduced income of the farmers'*. It was carried unanimously that *'the overseers be requested in answer to the letter of the Clerks of the Union to state to them that we have particularly examined the list of paupers of this parish and the amount of allowance now made to each of them, and find that no further reduction can be made in the same, and we do not know that they have any relations capable of contributing to their maintenance'.* It was also resolved *'that as the pay to the paupers during the last year forms only two thirds parts of the amount annually contributed to the Union by this parish, the Vestry strongly urges on the Board of Guardians the necessity of reducing the salaries of all the Officers of the Clutton Union which exceed those of Wells Union by nearly £300 per annum, and that they should be careful to restrict emergency allowances made to paupers, by the medical men, within reasonable bounds'.*

The people not receiving parish relief but in need of financial help were known as the 'second poor'. Both before and after the 1834 Act they received some help each year from the parish charities, which in the case of Hinton, had been set up by two compassionate women in the eighteenth century. In their wills they had made provision for the income from small fields that they owned to be used to relieve poverty among the parish residents. In1702, Mary Tegg, in her will, instructed that such rents were *'to be disposed of by the minister, churchwardens and overseers of the poor to such as had not weekly pay or constant relief'.* Ann Brookes in her will of 1791 left a field near Field Farm for her servant Hannah Hatch to benefit from during her lifetime and then she desired that *'her executors and the churchwardens should manure and let the said field to the advantage of poor families'.* The Charity Commission report (1819-1837) stated that the churchwardens had assured them that it was their intention to distribute the Ann Brookes Charity *'with a strict regard to the real wants and deserts of the poor, confining the benefits to those who are doing their best to maintain themselves independently of the parish relief, keeping a list of the persons to be relieved, in which list will be included only those who may be recommended by the respectable inhabitants of the parish'.* At the first Parish Meeting, in 1894, mention was made of the Church Bridge (Mary Tegg Charity) rent distribution and the income from another bequest of £100 that Captain John Roger Lawrence of Widcombe had made in favour of the poor of the parish. The income from the latter charity had apparently been used *'partly as a subscription to the Clothing Club, conducted for the benefit of the poor and the remainder put into a fund that had been raised by voluntary subscription for buying and distributing coal to the poor'*

After 1894 the Annual Assembly of the Parish Meeting took over considering the pauper list. Every year they paid 'doles' to needy families, from the Church Bridge Charity, and in 1911, for example, nine parishioners each received five shillings and sixpence halfpenny. Until 1927 the churchwardens and the overseers of the poor were actually responsible for distributing the money from the charities. Then, after the office of overseers was abolished, two charity trustees were nominated to take their place.

The working men had, since about 1839, been able to make some provision for themselves and their families in times of sickness, by joining the Hinton Club, a Benefit Society that has been mentioned in a previous chapter. That one reference is the only source of information that we have. How long it provided the chance of 'health insurance' we don't know or to which neighbouring village it was 'affiliated'. Temple Cloud Friendly Society was dissolved in the late 1860s but East Harptree continued into the beginning of the 1900s.

East Harptree Friendly Society. The photograph was probably taken after 1905, the year Mrs. Kettlewell presented the club with new spear-heads.

Times of Strife

Hinton Blewett did not escape the impact of the First World War, which claimed the lives of four men from the parish. The east window of the church is, in part, dedicated to them: William John Watts was the son of Edward and Emily Watts of Edgehill Farm, South Widcombe and although, the farm is just outside our parish boundary the family always worshipped here. William was a stoker on *H.M.S. Ariadne* and he died in action in July 1917 aged 20. He has no grave but is commemorated on the Plymouth War Memorial on The Hoe on panel 22. William John McArthur was in the 5th Battalion of the Queens Own Highlanders when he was killed in action, aged 30, at the Battle of Lys in April 1918. He was born in Battersea Middlesex but when he enlisted at Midsomer Norton in 1918 he was living at Sunnyside. He has no known grave but is commemorated on the Tyne Cot Memorial in Belgium on panel 136 to138. Stephen Stone was in the 60th

Battalion of the Machine Gun Corps (Infantry) when he died in Palestine in November 1918, aged 29. He was born at Wedmore, the son of Tom and Martha Stone, but he was living at Coley Hill Farm when he enlisted in Bristol. His grave is E 185 in the Kantara War Memorial Cemetery in Egypt. Herbert Stone was in the 2nd/5th Battalion, Gloucestershire Regiment in the Division that joined the 'Third battle of Ypres' and was killed, in action, during the struggle for the marshes below the Passchendaele Ridge. His body was never identified but he is honoured, along with nearly 35,000 others, on the Tyne Cot Memorial in Belgium, panel 72 to 75. As his name appears on the church window it is assumed that he had some connection with the parish. He enlisted, like William McArthur, at Midsomer Norton and it seems likely that he was related in some way to Stephen Stone. Fred Uphill came to live in the parish just after the war.

Fred Uphill (right) in his Royal Artillery uniform, during the First World War.

Once the war was over a committee was set up to organise a peace celebration in the parish, and a house-to-house collection was made to finance it. The celebrations began with the children, who had assembled on the Barbury, marching behind the Chew Valley Brass Band down to the schoolroom for tea. Afterwards they 'marched' back to join the adults in a field where they too were enjoying free refreshments. Sports followed for everyone, including a very exciting open event for adults that involved trying to catch a greased pig. Dorothy Bishop was the successful lady and Clifford Dury the successful gent. A waltzing competition was held during the evening to the accompaniment of the Brass Band. According to the *Somerset Guardian* '*the whole proceedings were a real success and a large crowd was in attendance*'. Afterwards, the organising committee discovered that after settling all the bills, including the £6 for the band, they were left with a balance of £6 5s 4d.

In 1939, as the likelihood of another major war became more certain, the parish Meeting discussed the subject of billeting and arrived at the conclusion that roughly 40 to 50 extra children could be housed in the village. They also reminded people that it was considered unpatriotic to store more than one week's supply of food.

The London evacuees, when they arrived at the schoolroom, were 'hand picked' by the waiting families, prepared to welcome them into their own homes. When Bristol was being blitzed, evacuee families from there came to the village too. Geoffrey Uphill recalled that his parents had at least a dozen extra people living at Sunnyside and that the presence of so many 'Townies' in the

The Chew Valley Brass Band (taken about eight years before they played at the Peace Celebrations here in the village).

A group of village and evacuee children at Prospect Stile in the 1940s. Left to right, standing; An unknown evacuee, Dennis Uphill, Geoffrey Uphill, Lilian Holloway, Hilda Uphill, Joyce Ford. Sitting; Vanda Cleveland, Irene Gillam, Stella Cleveland (three evacuees), June Holloway (partly hidden), Eileen Ford and Roma Cleveland (another evacuee).

village was both amusing and annoying. He said *"Most of them were terrified of animals and unlike the local 'kids' they didn't get a 'good clip round the ears' when they deserved it."* Bob and Connie Ford, of Upper Road, had a family of five sharing their house with them. Three of their own daughters slept at one end of a double bed in their sitting room and three evacuee girls slept at the other end. Audrey, their baby daughter slept in her cot beside the double bed.

Clifton Preparatory School, from Bristol, moved to the Manor accompanied by their headmaster, Mr. Moresby, and Miss Jones their matron. Church Ground, the field next to the churchyard, was their sports field and Basil Gibbons from Field Farm became one of the pupils.

In 1940 permission was given for a piece of land to be used as a scrap iron dump, but it seems that the District Council failed to collect it until after 1942. The dump was the likely destination for the iron railings that had been at the front of West End, Sunnyside and The Cottage.

Two volunteers from the village went, together, to Colston Street in Bristol, in May 1939 and joined the R.A.F. They were Jack Uphill and Harold Garland. Jack became an Air Frame Fitter and worked mainly on Spitfires, Hurricanes and Lancaster Bombers at a variety of Airbases around Britain and in North Africa and Italy. After six and a half years service he returned to Hinton Blewett and has lived here ever since. Harold Garland came safely through the war but never returned to live in the village. Jack's brother, Roy, was 'called up' to serve with the army but he was badly wounded in France at the D Day landings and was returned to a hospital in Liverpool. He came back to live in the village until the 1960s.

The members of the Home Guard included Graham Perry, Nelson Pool, Ron Bishop, Sidney Booy, Bill Andrews, Donald Harris, Bob Ford, Fred Uphill, Arthur Tyte, Trevor Payne, Geoffrey 'Pecker' King, 'Reg' Parker, Cecil Bishop, Arthur Blandford, Fred Dowling and Mr. Ousley, who was one of the evacuees from Bristol. They were organised with Harptree under the direction of Mr. Hancock of West Harptree shop. One day, when Donald Harris and Fred Dowling were on duty at the Home Guard hut along the Bishop Sutton

Jack Uphill, in his RAF uniform.

road, near the entrance to Whitehill Lane, a bomb fell nearby and Donald suffered a shrapnel injury to his arm. The 'Dad's Army' image of the Home Guard is fuelled by someone's recollection of the order, *"To the left, right turn"* being given as they practised their drill.

Hilda Selway remembers that Bill Andrews went around the village blowing two blasts on a whistle when an air raid was expected so that everyone had time to go to their 'shelter'. She and her siblings in the Uphill family were lucky because their father had built them a shelter in the garden. A great deal of trouble had been taken to make it as homely as possible including somehow covering the earth walls with wallpaper. But, despite all his effort, they never used it - because his wife couldn't be persuaded to go into it! The siren installed in the Manor cellar was never used either.

The ARPs checked that the 'blackout' was observed and that gas masks were issued. The chief warden was the rector, Walter Young, who was assisted by Cecil Leakey, Wyndham Andrews, John Garland and Fred Andrews. Cecil was living in Manor Cottage at the time and as soon as he reached down his hat to go out on patrol, his longhaired ginger cat would rush to his side. There the cat would stay as Cecil marched down to Widcombe, along to Coley, back to the village, along Hook Lane to Shortwood and home via Field Farm and Greenway. When Mr. Young joined the forces Cecil took over as chief warden.

About sixteen soldiers from the Northumberland Regiment were stationed at Blacknest Farm to 'man' the searchlight. Their huts were in the field, alongside the road, the Temple Cloud side of the farm buildings, under the elm trees. The searchlight was in the bottom of *'Stump'*, the large field on the opposite side of the road. When it was on, the light was so bright that Geoffrey Uphill remembers being able to count his carol singing money as he made his way around the village. Geoff's sister Hilda collected newspapers from Mr. Watts shop in Temple Cloud and delivered them to the soldiers as she cycled home from work at the 'Food Depot' near Cambrook House (the old Workhouse). She worked as part of the team that prepared 3,000 meals a day for the Bristol schoolchildren, which the W.R.V.S then transported in their vans to the various schools. The children were always given top priority for any food arriving at the City markets and only after their

Den Pool at the wheel of the bread delivery van in the 1940s. Cyril Church is standing beside the van with the breadbasket and moneybag. One headlamp has a blackout shield, and the house windows are taped over to avoid possible shatter damage in the event of an explosion.

needs had been catered for was any remaining food made available for sale in the shops.

Later in the war some Americans were posted to Hallatrow Court and it is said that the dozen Land Army girls billeted here at the Rectory soon attracted their attention. *"'T were like bees around a honey pot"* is still the phrase used. The girls didn't just attract Americans; one young Hinton Blewett farmer had already lost his heart to one that he had met at a Chew Magna dance. The young man was Arthur Herniman and 'Molly', as she became known, was the young lady. Molly was born Enid Mary Skells, and was living in Middlesex when she went to the Land Army Recruiting Centre in Oxford Street, London. She really wanted to join the Wrens but her mother forbade it, and as Molly said *"People did what their Mums said in those days"*. She had to wait until she was eighteen for a placement, which resulted in her leaving Paddington on a cold November day in 1941 with her large case, bound for Bristol Temple Meads. Her instructions were to make her way from there to Princes Street to catch a bus to West Harptree. As she struggled through the unfamiliar streets she noticed another girl with a large case who had also been on the crowded train, heading in the same direction. It transpired that they both caught the same bus to West Harptree to be met by James Gay with his father's horse and cart. The next morning when Molly woke at old Mrs. Small's cottage, near Widcombe Farm, she got her first view of the countryside that she had been unable to see in the darkness of the previous evening. She reported to the farm for duty and was dispatched, with one of James' jackets (because her uniform coat hadn't arrived) and a bottle of cold unsweetened tea, to help on the threshing machine. Not too long elapsed before she met Arthur at a dance in Chew Magna, and from then on he could be seen regularly, with his bike, making the journey to Widcombe, up and down the stony hill. His father had died and so, after a season of working for Colston Gay, Molly moved to Greenway Farm to help his mother, Clara Herniman, and her two sons on the farm.

Colston Gay had been so impressed by some ploughing that he had seen done with a tractor in 1936 that he bought a Fordson tractor and a Ransomes plough and Alfred, his son, who since he had left school in 1934 had been helping his father with the horses, very quickly learnt to manage the new machines. By 1937 farmers were being ordered to plough more ground - *'in case Hitler tried to starve us out'* and 'Alfie' was soon busy ploughing for many of the farms around. He clearly remembers ploughing fields along Whitehill and Hook Lane. With all the extra corn being grown, the farmers were clamouring for the services of someone with a threshing machine. Ernest Brown of Farrington Gurney owned a threshing machine that he had used locally since the First World War, but in 1941 he decided to sell it. Colston again 'kept ahead of the field' by astutely buying his own machine and Alfie was put in charge of it. The Agricultural Committee allocated him several parishes to work in, including Hinton Blewett, and both the machine and Alfie were kept very busy for many years. He still has his work journals for the year's 1942-1948, showing which farmers he threshed for, the amount of work he did and the charge made. He still has the threshing machine too! The farmers sold their wheat, or 'wit' as Alfie remembers Bobbie Masters of Coley Mill calling it, to the big companies like BOCM - after keeping a bit back for the hens! .

The engine from Ernest Brown's threshing machine was taken to Pensford Colliery to be used as a reserve engine in the event of a blitz that could result in miners being trapped underground.

It was that threshing machine that Molly forsook to come to Hinton Blewett and it was Alfie who changed her name for her. For some reason he didn't find 'Enid' an easy name to cope with, so it wasn't long before he, and Ben Hasell from Chew Magna, renamed her Molly - and Molly she has been, except to her family, ever since. Several years ago Molly wrote the following evocative piece for the Parish News and no attempt at recalling those days could be complete without it; *When I came from London to Hinton Blewett as a Land Army girl in 1943 it was a bustling, lively village. I think there were at least ten small farms clustered quite close together, one very smelly pig farm and a small ground of newish houses near the Barbury. Apart from the recently installed water and electricity and of course the wireless, I doubt life had changed much for generations.*

Most farmers had a hired help, a working wife and a good horse and coped well. The roads always seemed busy. Cows ambled slowly in from the fields for hand milking - and out again afterwards leaving the usual trail of cow pats for horses, pulling loaded carts, to spatter all over the lanes.

Butcher, Baker, and Oilman did their rounds. Oil lamps were still kept at the ready, as electricity could not be relied upon in the event of a storm. A small group of Council workers equipped with handcart, broom and tools worked continuously to keep the verges tidy. The verges were always full of flowers. No mechanical hedge-cutters then!

So when I was asked if I would take on the village milk round I was not in the least surprised to find myself balancing two brimming 5-gallon milk pails and a pint measure can on the handles of a very old bike! I had to start my round by pushing this load up the hill from Greenway Farm (just below the school - now the village hall) to the Ring of Bells at the top of the Barbury. Only once did disaster strike. This was on a wet and windy morning when, after the long push uphill and within a few steps of the top, I slipped. One can flew off the handles, bounced once, and then rolled back down the hill leaving a trail of fresh milk in its wake. With one can gone the bicycle handle swung round sharply and deposited the contents of the other 5-gallon can of milk all over my legs and feet. Not a good way to start a milk round!

However, normally it was an enjoyable trip round the village. Most people left their jugs ready on the kitchen table. Doors were never locked in those days! All were given full measure with a drop extra for the cat. Mrs. Wall, then the landlady of the Ring of Bells greeted me at least once a week with "Why don't you go home before you get stuck here for life?" She thought all farmers were slave- drivers and made no secret of it. Old Mr. Booy, who lived in the cottage next door to the pub, waited - jug in hand - every morning to give me a further instalment of "What I did in the Boer War", a saga which lasted all one summer.

I got to know all the villagers very well. In those days everyone seemed to have time to stop and chat. When I became a farmer's wife I didn't regret being "stuck here for life" one little bit.

Margery Leakey did her bit to help the war effort and earned a little bit of extra money by doing 'outwork'. She did what she called "rubbers" and that involved cycling to Ford, near Chewton Mendip and collecting 2 feet 6 inch long bundles of cables. The ends of each bundle of 25 insulated cables had to be very carefully prepared. At one end of the cable, one inch had to be cut from the outer rubber coating and half an inch of the insulation removed from the three inner wires. The other end had to have half an inch taken off the outer casing and a quarter of an inch from the inner wires. There was a bonus for anyone completing 1,000 cables a week! Pansy Norris from Coley Hill Farm used to come up with her horse and trap to pick up Hilda Uphill before they set off to do their bit for the war effort. They collected waste paper from around the village and took it to the barn at West End Farm from where Mrs. James arranged for it to be collected.

A minute from the 1946 Parish Meeting reported that *'owing to the special difficulties of providing food and the trouble and expense that would be involved, the plan for victory celebrations for the children on June 8th were to be dropped - there would be instead a special service of thanksgiving'*. Their reasons for coming to that decision gives us an invitation to reflect on the affect that the war had had on this very small, rural, close and hard working community.

Faces and Places

Before leaving this glimpse of Hinton Blewett, we hope you enjoy the following small selection from the photographs we have of the people and 'their' village in those days. We hope too that you will forgive us for any errors we have inadvertently made in identifying them. We look forward to your help in correcting any mistakes, to any additional information you may be able to provide, and to receiving any copies of photographs that will help us to build up an even better picture of 'days gone by'.

Adults, Edward Gibbons (left) and William Holloway with their families, sometime around 1913. In the cart, (l-r), Unknown, Wilfred Gibbons, Douglas Tucker and Bevis Tucker. Standing - Dennis Gibbons with William (Bill) Holloway behind him, 'Nan' Holloway, Hilda Holloway in the arms of Olive Holloway, probably another Holloway, and perhaps Flo' Holloway.

The Reverend J. H. Johnson outside the church in 1910 (approx). A small branch of the yew tree that was at the rear of the Ring of Bells is visible top left.

The wedding of George Herniman and Clara Jones in the early 1900s. The Jones family lived in cottages that were opposite The Lodge.

The wedding of Margery Summers (great-niece of Clara Jones) and Cecil Leakey. They married on the 3rd September 1939 - the day that war broke out.

'Bob' Ford and his wife 'Connie' in the 1920s. They lived at Thimble Cottage before moving to the new Council houses when they were built on Upper Road.

Samuel Cook and his wife. Samuel was born in Hinton Blewett in 1828, the son of William and Keziah. He emigrated to Australia in 1849, married in 1855 and died in 1902.

The young members of the Perry family in 1907/8. Beginning with the youngest they are; Albert, Annie, Graham, Amy, Henry and Marie. The photo' was taken at what is now known as Greenway Cottage but was then Greenway Farm.

William Holloway in about 1900. He lived at Sedbrook Farm, The Ring of Bells where he was a carpenter as well as the landlord and at Elmgrove Farm.

An eary 1930s photo taken on the Barbury of Harry Andrews, Arthur Bishop and Johnny (Jack) Pool. The objects at their feet are their caps.

Sidney Booy and Wyndham Andrews (wearing gaiters) with Charlie Gay's dog in the 1930s outside Manor Cottage garden.

Wilfred Gibbons from Field Farm. He was the father of Eric who now lives at Sedbrook Farm.

Twins, Mary and William (Bill) Andrews at Hillside Cottage.

Ron Bishop with Bob and Captain at Blacknest Farm.

Monica Small - later Andews in the early 1900s. She was in service with Charlie Gay and spent her married life at Greenway Cottage.

Blacknest Farm with Harry Andrews and the bull in the foreground.

A rather indistinct photo' of The Ring Of Bells taken around the turn of the twentieth century. The young boy is Phillip Golding who was visiting the village with his parents. His father was the landlord of the Carpenters Arms, Dundry and Phillip's grandparents were Mr. and Mrs. Toghill who had lived at West House and were buried here in the churchyard. It is just possible to see, on the left, that the horse is enjoying a snack from a wheelbarrow and, on the right, the outside stairs to the clubroom.

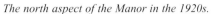
The north aspect of the Manor in the 1920s.

Eliza Lyons, in about 1909, with her daughter and stepdaughter at what is now known as Greenway Farm.

West End Farm and the Tucker Family in 1907.

West House Farm, now a Grade II listed building, sometime around the mid 1920s.

The cottage that was opposite The Cottage. The plaque above its door bears the date 1799. It was derelict for many years before finally being demolished in the 1960s.

Harry and Annie Bishop with two of their children, Cecil and Dorothy, at Middle Road Farm.

Ann Rawlings outside Abbots Barn Farm around the turn of the twentieth century.

69

Dates of some of the villagers mentioned in the text.

Andrews, Bill, 1910-1983
Andrews, Fred', 1903-1972
Andrews, Harry, 1907-1984
Andrews, Monica (Small), 1892-1978
Andrews, Wyn', 1905-1972
Bishop, Harry, 1875-1954
Booy, Seward, 1908-1988
Booy, Sid', c1907-1965
Diamond, Bert', 1899-1974
Diamond, Fred', 1905-1980
Diamond, Mary (Andrews), 1910-1994
Diamond, Priscilla (Holloway), 1914-1967
Ford, Bob, 1905-1967
Ford, Connie, 1906-2001
Gay, Dorothy (Board), 1913-2003
Gay, Gordon, 1905-1993
Gibbons, Dennis, 1907-1936
Gibbons, Edward, 1874-1947
Harris, Don', 1918-1966
Harris, Greta (Evans), 1906-1992
Harris, Wilfred, 1896- 1974

Herniman, Arthur, 1918-1979
Herniman, Clara (Jones), 1882-1951
Herniman, George, 1885-1941
Herniman, Maurice, 1912-1984
Holloway, Alice (Rawlings) - 'Grandma', 1873-1947
Holloway, Bill, 1902-1970
Holloway, Lilian, 1895-1971
Holloway, William, 1859-1934
Leakey, Cecil, 1913-1997
Lyons, Alfie, 1898-1985
Lyons, Andrew, 1854-1937
Pool, Dennis, 1912-1999
Pool, Nelson, 1908-1975
Pool, Rossiter, 1866-1938
Redwood, Henry, 1833-1906
Spear, 'Lammy', 1836-1925
Stokes, Frances (Lyons), 1890-1966
Uphill, Fred, 1889-1964
Uphill, Martha, 1895-1972
Watts, Alfie, 1901-1988
Watts, May, 1906-2001
Weaver, Lester, c1898-1960

Acknowledgements

This publication is the culmination of many years of interest in, curiosity about and research, into Hinton Blewett. As the result of initial enthusiasm among a group of residents, a series of evening classes was held in the village hall, researching village history under the guidance of Dr. Lee Prosser. We are especially grateful to him for his help, encouragement and interest, which continued for many years after the course finished. A Rural Action grant enabled the formation of the history group, which could then continue with its researches and organise a programme of talks each year.

I would like to thank fellow members of the history group for the work and contributions that they have made over the years, in particular Pat Baldwin, Liz Brimmell, Michael Browning, Michael Flower, Gill Hogarth, Veronica Otley, Graham Sage, Vernon Smith, John Tansley, Roger Wilcox and Bob Williams.

We are all particularly grateful to the staff at Somerset Records Office, the Local Studies Library and the local libraries, for their patience and guidance.

The Countryman magazine gave their permission for the use of Brian Walker's illustrations and he also provided additional artwork in the form of illustrations and work on the maps.

I would like to thank Bill and Lynn Blanning for the information they supplied about those parishioners who lost their lives in the First World War and David S.D. Jones for information gleaned from his booklet *'The Cambrook House Story'*. I am also indebted to Lord Rees-Mogg for his readiness to allow me to use photographs and information from his family collection.

Most importantly I would like to thank all the people who willingly gave their time and shared their recollections and photographs with us; Kathleen Andrews, Wilfred Beer, Audrey Bird (née Ford), Seward Booy, Kathleen Bowden (née Stokes), Cliff and Charles Bown, Mrs. Clarke of Clutton, Bertram Cook, Rodney Cook, Yvonne Crossman (née Wookey), Mary Diamond (née Andrews), Dorothy and Gordon Gay, Eric Gibbons, Joyce Harris (née Hann), Gwen Herniman, Molly Herniman, Veronica Hummell, Cecil and Margery Leakey, Evangeline Lewis, Frederick Long, June Maggs (née Holloway), Theodore Maidment, Joyce Millard (née Stokes), Dennis Pool, Heather Pool, Betty Ponting (née Shepherd), Lord Rees-Mogg, Lilian Richards (née Holloway), Hilda Selway (née Uphill), Jack Uphill, May Watts and Joan Wiles.

Many of these people are, sadly, no longer with us, and I hope that this book might serve as a tribute to them. My sincere apologies to anyone that I have inadvertently forgotten to thank. I assure them that the omission is quite unintentional.

On a personal note, I would like to mention Watch, our dog; who was my enthusiastic companion on explorations that took us into every corner of the parish and along every mile of hedgerow. I am also grateful for all the help and direction I have received from Roy Gallop and Ken Griffiths of Fiducia Press.
.

Quality Books
from Fiducia Press

LOCAL HISTORY........
A Celebration of the Avon New Cut - 60 pages, 84 fine illustrations. **£7**
Parrett River Trade - Barging on the Parrett, Yeo and Westport Canal. **£5**
Workhouse - A glimpse of the Poor Law and the Clutton Workhouse - **£2**
Healing Waters - Somerset's many mineral springs and small spas. **£4**
Fussells Ironworks, Mells - A full and detailed account 1744-1895. **£5**
The Glastonbury Canal - The illustrated history of a lost Somerset water route to the sea at Highbridge. **£5**
The Coaching Era - The colourful days of stage and mail coach travel in Somerset, Bath and Bristol. **£6.50**
The Gentle Giants - The story of a Bristol family timber haulage business and its Shire Horses. **£3**

PAST SOMERSET TIMES
An occasional series filled with high-interest, wide ranging studies from Somerset's rich history, presented in a well-designed and highly readable form. Volume 2, **£5**, Volume 3, **£6**

POETRY..........
Orra: A Lapland Tale - William Barnes' poignant poetry originally published in 1822. **£7**
Tracts from the Tracks - Mark Griffiths' Ridgeway poems. **£5**
Manly Monodes - 20 clever and alliterative poems by the Scottish poet Tom Lamb. **£5**
Poetical Pieces - A collection of remarkable early poems by the Dorset poet William Barnes. **£6**

PLACES AND PEOPLE
Exploring the Smaller Towns of Somerset - history, walks, gazetteer, photographs and maps. **£5**

MUSIC........
Dave Collett Blues - A varied selection of words and music. **£5**

RAILWAYS.......
Great Railway Battles - Twenty dramatic confrontations between the early railway companies. **£10**

The Severn Tunnel - A vivid account of the 1872-1887 construction by the tunnel's own engineer. **£15**
GWR Reflections - an enthralling 144 pages, with 291 photos. **£10**

SPECIAL TITLES
Views of Labour and Gold - Reprint of William Barnes' 1859 writings on political and moral economy with a new and detailed introduction. **£10**
Georgia Meets the Railway Goblins - Colourful presentation of a magical story for children of all ages. **£5**

FORTHCOMING BOOKS:
Miners' Memories of the South Bristol Coalfield
Hghway Robbery A brief look at Highwaymen and Highwaywomen

All orders are post free. Bulk order terms 40% discount (minimum any 4 books) Cheque or Postal order made payable to Fiducia Press 10 Fairfield Road, Bristol BS3 1LG or telephone 0117 9482795, 0117 971 3609 or 01934 631616 Also: www,bristolpublishers.co.uk